THE GIRL WHO SAID NO TO THE NAZIS

SOPHIE SCHOLL AND THE PLOT AGAINST HITLER

HOW SOPHIE AND HER FRIENDS
STOOD UP FOR WHAT THEY BELIEVED

© Dan Paton

Haydn Kaye has loved history since he was very young. His mother helped to spark his interest by telling him what it was like to be a child during World War Two, and ever since then he's often wondered how he might have acted if he'd lived in Germany under the Nazis. He went on to study history at Oxford University, before teaching and writing about historical subjects ranging from the pyramids to the Olympics, and from Queen Elizabeth I to writer Roald Dahl.

His latest books for younger readers have been the life stories of Emmeline Pankhurst and Albert Einstein.

His website is www.haydnmiddleton.com.

SOPHIE SCHOLL AND THE PLOT AGAINST HITLER

HAYDN KAYE
With illustrations by Amerigo Pinelli

PUSHKIN CHILDREN'S

Pushkin Press
71–75 Shelton Street
London WC2H 9JQ

First published in the UK by Pushkin Press in 2020

1 3 5 7 9 8 6 4 2

ISBN 13: 978-1-78269-275-1

Designed and typeset by Tetragon, London
Printed and bound by CPI Group (UK) Ltd, Croydon, CR0 4YY

www.pushkinpress.com

THE GIRL WHO SAID NO TO THE NAZIS

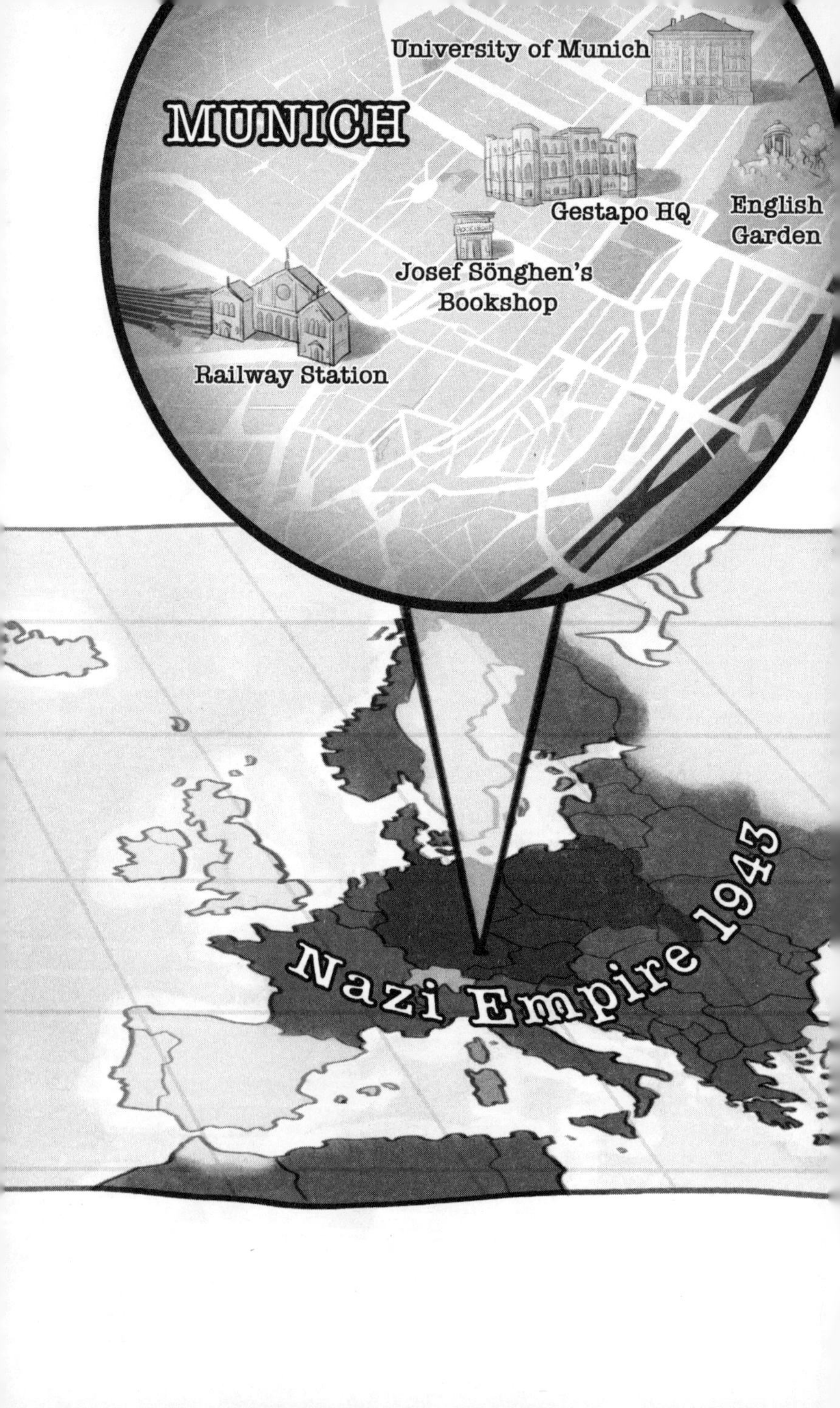
University of Munich
MUNICH
Gestapo HQ
English Garden
Josef Sönghen's Bookshop
Railway Station
Nazi Empire 1943

BERLIN SPORTS PALACE, GERMANY

18TH FEBRUARY 1943

The man in the spotlight kept shaking his fist. He seemed to hate the air so much he was trying to punch a hole in it, and although he was tiny and frail, his magnified voice could have woken the dead.

He was Joseph Goebbels, right-hand man to Germany's *Führer*, or leader, Adolf Hitler. Their National Socialist Party, nicknamed the Nazis, had been running the country for ten years; for more than three they'd been heading for victory in World War Two. It was surely just a matter of time before the Nazis conquered the planet.

'I ask you,' little Goebbels roared. 'Will you follow our *Führer* through thick and thin in the struggle to win this war?'

'*Ja!*' came the deafening reply from all fifteen thousand Germans seated in front of him. Yes!

'Do you want a war more total than anything we can even imagine today?'

'*Ja! Ja!*'

'Do you agree that everyone who goes against the war effort in any way should pay for it with his head?'

'*Ja! Ja! Ja!*'

On it went.

As the men and women in the audience bellowed their answers, many leaped to their feet and shot out their right arms in the fearsome Nazi salute. So did millions more beyond the arena listening in on their radios. From the highest-ranking German army officer to the humblest German nurse or postman, no matter what the Nazis asked for, there could only be one reply:

Ja!

Six hundred kilometres away to the south, a fresh-faced first-year student at the University of Munich was posing for an official photo. Elsewhere in the building, the storm of noise on the radio grew louder and louder:

Ja! Ja! Ja! Ja! Ja! Ja! Ja!...

The girl stared into the lens, disgusted by all she heard.

'*Nein,*' she said under her breath as the camera flashed.

No.

NINE MONTHS EARLIER

A CITY IN HITLER'S GERMANY

Sophie Scholl stepped down from the train.

In one hand she carried a suitcase, in the other a box on a string. The box held a home-baked cake and two bottles of wine, because that night there was going to be a double celebration. Here at the start of May 1942 Sophie was about to reach the grand old age of twenty-one. That was exciting enough, but maybe even more excitingly, and quite unusually for a girl, she was also about to enrol at the University of Munich.

The smoke from all the standing trains was so thick it hid the high roof of Munich Main Station. Closer to the ground it made the milling crowds look like ghosts – ghosts for the most part in uniform: regular-army grey, Stormtrooper brown, the black of the elite Security Corps. Even civilians wore small metal swastikas on their lapels or as cufflinks to show they were loyal to the Nazis.

But however hard Sophie searched among them, she couldn't see her elder brother Hans, and that was a serious disappointment.

Hans was already studying in Munich to be a doctor. He'd promised to meet Sophie, but outside of lectures and hospital duties he had to be on standby as an army sergeant. Already he'd served in a medical support team in the victory over France; now he must have got his marching orders again, maybe this time to the Russian Front, where their younger brother Werner was also headed.

Setting off along the platform to the ticket barrier, Sophie tried her best not to feel let down. Orders were orders – everyone had to obey. But who could she now share her cake and wine with? It might have been better to stay on a little longer in Ulm, her home city, and celebrate with her parents and two older sisters.

When she remembered that big sunny apartment on the cathedral square, for a moment she half wished she hadn't left it at all.

A long queue had formed at the barrier. It wasn't just tickets that had to be checked but ID too, and a small white-haired woman up ahead was having trouble producing the right papers. With a sigh

Sophie set down her suitcase and box and, hoping against hope, continued to scan the crowds for Hans.

She knew she too was being watched. Everyone was – all the time.

One passer-by after another shot her a suspicious look, glancing down at her luggage as if she might be carrying something she shouldn't. In Adolf Hitler's Germany it was so easy to seem disloyal. They treated you like a criminal just for making an anti-Nazi joke, and, judging from the way some of these people were looking at Sophie, they could even read anti-Nazi thoughts.

Standing very upright in her baggy mannish coat, she might have attracted attention anyway. Not many girls her age looked the way she did. The frown on her pale round face made her appear more careworn than someone twice as old, but the daisy she'd tucked behind her ear – a bright splash of yellow and white against the brown of her shoulder-length hair – made her seem almost childlike.

Still no one moved in the queue. Then suddenly out of the smoky shadows a pair of men in dark suits and hats hurried across to the barrier. A shiver passed down the line.

'*Gestapo!*' The Nazis' dreaded secret state policemen.

Within moments they were frogmarching the poor older woman away, and only then did Sophie spot on

the left-hand side of her coat the six-pointed yellow star which the Nazis made all Jews wear as a badge of humiliation, as if being Jewish was a crime in itself.

Sophie felt so sorry for the woman, yet utterly, utterly helpless – because however keen you were to stand up to these Nazis, it would have been easier to stop one of their terrifying tanks with your little finger.

Now all the other ticket-holders passed through into the station forecourt. To remind herself of the route she had to take, Sophie unfolded the map Hans had drawn for her. It was a thirty-minute walk to the university buildings. But on folding away the piece of paper, she heard quick footsteps coming up behind her. A second later, a hand clamped down hard on her shoulder.

Sophie froze. You never knew when your own turn would come. What had she said? What had she done? Who had informed on her?

But as she turned around, she heard the magic word: 'Sophia!'

Her face broke apart in the widest, most beautiful grin. Only one person ever called her by her unshortened name. The person she adored above all others.

'Hans!' She flung her arms around her brother and buried her face in his chest.

Briefly Hans and Sophie clung together as if for dear life.

Then each drew back to size the other up. Neither said much: the most innocent words could be overheard and used against you. But a single look told Sophie all she needed to know. Here was her Hans: as tall, dark, fit and handsome as ever; and if you could actually look clever, then Hans looked clever too. Just one thing was missing from the usual picture – an eye-catching girl on his arm.

Hans half turned from his sister and beckoned another person forward.

'Sophia,' he said. 'There's someone I couldn't keep away.'

Sophie laughed as an impossibly elegant young woman stepped up to shake her hand. It was Traute, a medical student friend of Hans whom she'd met before and really liked, though the two of them now were plainly more than just good friends.

'Birthday girl!' Traute said. 'You're going to have the time of your life here in Munich!'

Hans had already picked up Sophie's suitcase and box and was striding towards the street exit. 'Follow me,' he called back. 'The party's at my place.'

Sophie and Traute exchanged grins, linked arms and set off behind him.

DANGEROUS TALK

'So let's see if I've got all your names straight,' said Sophie, and her five party guests, none of them older than twenty-four, lined up in front of her.

For a moment she shut her eyes to order her thoughts, then she pointed at the only other girl in Hans's lodgings.

'Traute,' Sophie declared with a smile.

Hans's girlfriend smiled back and squeezed Sophie's finger. 'Correct!'

Sophie moved along to three clean-cut young men. When introducing them, Hans had said all three were soldier-students like him, and all in training to be doctors. They all towered over Sophie too.

'You,' she said to the tallest, who also seemed the gentlest, 'are Christel.'

'At your service, madam,' he replied with a nod and a little bow.

'And you,' Sophie went on to the next boy, a lively athletic type with a pipe clamped between his teeth, 'are Schurik.'

'Delighted to make your acquaintance, ma'am!'

She came to the broad-shouldered third. 'Which must mean you're Willi.'

'I guess it must,' he agreed in a deadpan way, and the others all laughed. Sophie liked Willi as much as any of them, but she still hadn't seen him smile.

'And how about me?' asked Hans playfully. 'Who am I?'

Sophie flipped his shoulder. 'You? Ah well, you could be anyone. Who's ever going to remember *your* name!'

The party could hardly have gone better. They ate Sophie's cake and drank her wine, polished off the few other bits of food and drink they'd saved from their rations, and afterwards sat in a circle singing songs accompanied by Hans's guitar and Schurik's balalaika. Then Willi called for silence.

'I have a joke,' he said, to Sophie's surprise, since Willi didn't exactly seem like a comedian. 'Hitler pays a visit to his troops at the Russian Front—'

'Well, that's not going to happen for a start!' Schurik cut in, still sucking on his pipe though it had long since gone out. 'Everyone knows our *Führer* sends us there to die in our thousands, but wouldn't go near the place himself.'

'Quiet, Schurik. This is part of the joke. So: our *Führer* goes to see his loyal troops at the Front – to lift morale, you know? – and he says to an infantryman, "If a Russian bomb should land nearby, what would be your dying wish?"' Willi paused for effect before his punchline. 'The infantryman replies, "I would wish for my *Führer* to be standing beside me."'

Nobody laughed; the tension in the room became electric and Sophie knew all eyes were on her. This was a test. They wanted to know just how anti-Nazi the new girl was. Would she disapprove of such dangerous talk? Might she even feel she had to report Willi?

Sophie's dark eyes lit up. 'That's brilliant!' she giggled. 'Let's hope the infantryman gets his wish!'

Then everyone else started chuckling with relief.

'See what I told you,' said Hans. 'She's one of us.'

After that, Hans's friends talked more openly but more nervously about the Nazi Party that ruled over them. 'Senseless', they called the horrific world war it had unleashed, 'needless', 'criminal'.

'You know we can't hope to win?' Christel said to Sophie. 'How can we ever beat all the Allies – not just the British, but the Americans and Russians too?'

'We refuse to call the Allies "the enemy",' Traute explained to her. 'Our truest enemy is Hitler.'

'I hope they do defeat us,' added Schurik, who'd earlier said he was half-Russian himself. 'Then once they've blitzed those Nazi creeps, the rest of us can all go back to normal.'

'How about you, Sophie?' asked Willi. 'How do you feel about this war?'

Sophie opened her mouth to speak, but her brother beat her to it: 'Oh, this is a girl who used to cry for hours on end if she saw a mouse caught in a trap!'

Sophie nodded. 'I don't believe in violence of any kind. We can't base our lives on brute force.' She looked around the circle. 'But what can people like us actually do? To show we're opposed to everything the Nazis stand for?'

'Nothing,' said Hans, rather too quickly. 'There's absolutely nothing any of us can do.'

Sophie saw him throw a kind of warning look at the others. As if in response, Traute jumped to her feet. 'This is unhappy talk for a party!' she said. 'Why don't we all take a moonlight stroll?'

Together they walked to a local park called the English Garden. With the twin domes of the great cathedral looming dark against the night sky, they sat by the River Isar and carried on chatting.

Willi, Sophie learned, had already served on the Russian Front. Christel had a young family – and neither soldier Willi nor airman Christel was stationed in Munich itself but travelled in to study at the university. Fellow medic Traute was based even further away, in Hamburg, but came down to Munich for extra courses.

'So will you follow your brother into doctoring, Sophie?' she asked.

Sophie shook her head. 'I'll probably settle for being a kindergarten teacher. I trained as a children's nurse before I had to do my national service. I just wanted to come here first to stretch my mind a little.'

'Then what exactly will you be studying?' asked Schurik.

'Philosophy and biology.'

At that, Willi's ears pricked up. 'Philosophy? Make sure you attend the lectures of Professor Kurt Huber. He is *very good*.'

He said the last two words in a slow flat way. Since coming outdoors – where even the bushes could have ears – Sophie had noticed all four of the men in particular do this at times, almost as if certain words or phrases were a code for something else.

'Come now,' said Hans, springing to his feet. 'We must be getting back. Our brand-new student here needs her beauty sleep!'

Sophie gave a tired, happy sigh. 'Thank you all so much for tonight,' she told her brother and his lovely gang. 'I'll never forget this birthday party.'

'Your first as an official grown-up,' said Christel. 'Many happy returns!'

TO LIVE A GOOD LIFE

Sophie arrived early at the Auditorium Maximum to make sure she got a ringside seat.

Willi had been right: as a lecturer, Professor Kurt Huber was very good indeed. The mornings when Sophie came to hear him talk were the highlights of her week, and plenty of others felt the same way. Today, yet again, there had to be nearly 250 students awaiting his arrival – the vast majority of them young men.

They didn't all stop chattering as the Prof entered. Short and grey-haired, he had limped since he was a boy, and he didn't find it easy to climb the rostrum. Once he was standing in position, he stared dead ahead until there was total silence.

Then he gave a cough to clear his throat, but when he began his lecture, it sounded for all the world as if he was still coughing. Until his voice had warmed up, the same childhood illness which had damaged his leg still made it hard for him to talk. Some of the more unkind students shared silent smiles.

Sophie took no notice. Already she was devoting her entire attention to his marvellous words.

'Philosophy' means 'love of wisdom' and the Prof certainly made his listeners fall in love with the wisdom of history's greatest thinkers. Many of these thinkers were German: men who'd lived in a nobler German Fatherland whose people would have despised the Nazis.

Traute had said the Prof was an expert on old German folk songs as well as philosophy, and it was obvious to Sophie that he loved his country deeply, but that didn't mean he loved Hitler. 'To live a good life,' he once said when discussing a philosopher from two centuries before, 'people must think, not just obey without question.' That sounded to Sophie like a dig at the Nazis. Another time, after discussing a genius from even longer ago, he snorted, 'But this man was Jewish, so watch out in case he poisons your mind!'

That gave Sophie a jolt. Professors seldom made jokes about the Nazis' hatred of the Jews – not if they valued their jobs or their lives. A few years before, members of this university had even organized a public bonfire for piles of 'un-German' books to be thrown on the flames. So it thrilled Sophie to hear the wheezy old lecturer hinting that things had gone horribly wrong in Germany. It worried her too, because dotted around the auditorium were plenty of *Spitzel* – Student Association spies of Sophie's age who were only too happy to report 'disloyalty' of any kind.

As that morning's lecture neared its end, Sophie looked up from her note-taking after the Prof read out a line written by the philosopher Gottfried Leibniz:

'*He who does not act does not exist.*'

The words came from three centuries earlier, but Sophie didn't believe the Prof was talking only about the past. She was sure she saw defiance in his tired old eyes as he let the words sink in.

She was still mulling this over when she saw Hans just in front of her in the queue to leave the auditorium. They embraced and walked together out into the June sunshine to find a coffee shop.

'So you medics are sent to learn philosophy too!' said Sophie.

'The Prof is always worth a listen,' Hans replied. 'I met him recently too, at Schurik's father's house, and we talked.' Seeming a little on edge, he looked around carefully as they crossed a grassy open space where a fountain splashed. 'I was watching you in there,' he went on in a lower tone. 'You looked up when he quoted Leibniz.'

'*He who does not act does not exist*?' Sophie kept her own voice soft.

Hans gave a strange brisk nod. It somehow managed to communicate three separate things: firstly, that Sophie should keep this to herself; secondly, that yes, Hans too had picked up a possibly coded message; which meant that, thirdly, the Prof might well be another person whose opinions made him 'one of them'.

'He is brave, though,' Sophie murmured. 'With so many spies in the room.'

'Ah, those donkeys!' Hans grunted. 'They're all too dim to understand!'

They picked the wrong cafe in the nearby Schwabing district.

Soon after they ordered, a crowd of rowdy fellow-students piled into the place, greeting one another with the 'Heil Hitler' salute and yelling as if in a gale. Their mere presence seemed to make Hans more jittery still.

Like so many at the university, these young men could never, ever, be mistaken for 'one of them'. Sophie imagined their sort queuing up to fuel that bonfire of books, some written by Heinrich Heine, a

Jewish author whose poems always lifted her heart. *Where they burn books*, her beloved Heine had chillingly warned a century earlier, *they will also in the end burn human beings*.

All the boys' loud talk was of the war, but it sounded as if they were discussing a different conflict from the one Hans and Sophie so loathed. They had no doubt the German 'master race' would soon capture the key city of Stalingrad and defeat the Russians, even though the invasion was taking months longer than scheduled.

Then one of the few girls with them risked mentioning the air-raid shelters being built all over Munich. For years Nazi bombers had laid waste to Allied cities; now 'enemy' planes were making raids on the Fatherland, and the western city of Cologne in particular had taken some massive hits. The girl began to suggest this might make things tougher, but one of her group interrupted.

'Don't talk like such a loser!' he yelled. 'Under the *Führer*, we cannot be defeated! For every bomb the enemy drops on us, we'll simply drop two back!'

'Hey,' another jeered at her. 'You're not one of these White Rose traitors, are you?'

'White Flag, more like! Those cowards just want to surrender!'

Sophie frowned across the table at Hans, asking him with her eyes what 'White Rose' might mean. He replied with a shrug and quickly bolted down the last of his coffee.

Sophie leaned in closer. 'No, tell me, Hans,' she pressed him. 'You do know, don't you? What is this White Rose?'

'It's nothing. Just a stupid, pointless thing you should steer well clear of.' He jumped to his feet and glanced around like a man on the run. 'Now drink up and let's go. This place really stinks.'

A CALL TO REVOLT

Not long after sunrise a well-built man in his mid-forties approached his fortress-like office building on Munich's Brienner Street, just a few minutes away from the English Garden.

Carrying a leather briefcase and smoking a cigarette, he was Gestapo interrogator Robert Mohr – and since he never switched off his internal radar for a second, he'd already spotted an older, heavier stranger lurking in the shadows.

The man now stepped forward with a greeting of 'Heil Hitler!' Despite his great bulk, his voice was high and shrill.

'Heil Hitler,' Mohr replied, eyeing him from under the brim of his hat, then walking on, only for the man to fall into step beside him.

'Sir, I do not wish to take more than a minute of your time,' he panted. 'But, dear sir, may I ask if you work in this place?' He gestured up at the four-storey building which had once been a royal palace, though now as everyone knew it was the Gestapo's city headquarters.

Mohr shot him another, colder look, but still didn't speak or pause. So the bulky man, gasping for breath, reached into his trouser pocket and pulled out a crumpled envelope. 'The thing is, sir, I should like to hand in this.'

At that, Mohr tossed away his cigarette butt and turned to face him.

'Sir,' the man began to babble. 'I found it in my mailbox. I swear to God I do not know where it came from. I think it was maybe sent to me as a foul joke? Or maybe to test my loyalty – to see if I would do my duty and hand it in? Which is what I would like to do now, sir. Right away.'

He held out the envelope as if it was a small verminous animal. Mohr took it and studied the neatly typed words on the front.

'This is your name and address?' he asked, without looking up.

'It is, sir. As you see, sir, my wife and I run a little café in the old town. I need, in fact, to be getting back to our kitchen right away. I have many breakfasts to serve. My wife, working alone, will soon be rushed off her feet and—'

'Hold your tongue,' said Mohr, setting down his briefcase on the pavement between his feet. 'Please.'

Then he opened the envelope, which carried a Munich postmark, and took out two folded sheets of paper densely covered with print.

They could have been pages torn from a book, but Mohr saw at once they'd been written on a typewriter and then copied. He checked the first and last lines. Headed Leaflets of the White Rose, the text ended not with a signature but the words: *Please make as many copies of this leaflet as possible and pass them on*.

Having read that much, Mohr skimmed through the rest without delay, and what he found was different from anything he had seen in ten years as a Gestapo officer, or in the fourteen before that working for the local state police.

It was like an essay. The kind university tutors set for their students. There were even two sections copied out of a book by someone called Lao-Tzu, an author Mohr hadn't heard of and who didn't sound particularly German.

'A foul joke', the man in front of him had called it – a man now visibly sweating and wringing his hands while holding his tongue as ordered. It would take a sick sense of humour to laugh at some of these typed words.

The *Führer* and the National Socialist Party were described as *a gang of criminals*. The whole Nazi movement *depended on the deception and betrayal of one's fellow man* and *could support itself only by constant lies*, while carrying out the murders of 300,000 Jews in Poland alone since that country was conquered.

Why are the German people so uncaring in the face of all these abominable crimes? the nameless typist demanded. *Crimes so unworthy of the human race.*

Mohr's hand tightened on the sheets when he re-read the sentence that had struck him like a blow to the back of his head:

Now that we have recognized them for what they are, it must be the sole and first duty, the holiest duty of every German, to destroy these Nazi beasts.

Incredible as it might seem, this was a call to rise up in revolt!

Mohr replaced the leaflet in the envelope, slid it into the inner pocket of his jacket and looked up. The café-owner was now close to tears.

'I swear to you on the life of my children, good sir,' he pleaded, 'I am horrified by what is written there! I didn't even read it all the way through! I brought it straight here, sir, as anyone who loves our *Führer* would.'

He wanted to go on but Mohr held up his hand. 'Yet it was to you they sent it. Why would they have done this?'

The man repeated his claim that he had no idea, and again, his voice beginning to crack, he suggested it might all be a joke in the worst possible taste. Meanwhile more early-morning workers were appearing on Brienner Street. Most looked the other way when they saw the dispute going on outside the huge sinister building: Gestapo interrogators didn't have to wear uniforms to identify themselves – even the surrounding air seemed to shrink away from them.

Mohr let the man finish. As it happened, he believed what he was hearing. You didn't rise to his rank without being able to smell a liar. It was possible that one of Mohr's colleagues really had mailed out the traitorous leaflet to random owners of cafés and beer halls – the sort of place where such a thing might easily be passed around – just to see who turned it in and who didn't.

But to the Gestapo, every citizen was suspect, and while this café-owner might be wholly innocent, in his panic he might still incriminate others.

'You have your own papers with you?' asked Mohr, reaching for his briefcase and indicating a street door further along the wall. 'Then please come with me.'

'What – into the building?' The man sounded petrified. People who went in there sometimes didn't come out. 'No, sir, as I mentioned, I must now return to my work. And besides, I have told you absolutely everything I know—'

With a look that could pierce leather, Mohr struck him silent. 'Your wife shall serve breakfast alone this morning. Come with me.'

'YOU ARE THE WHITE ROSE!'

It wasn't the most gripping hour Sophie had ever spent.

This biology lecturer was no Kurt Huber, and Sophie's attention kept wandering to some grubby typewritten sheets folded together on the floor under the next empty desk. She half wished she could read what was typed on them – it could hardly be less interesting than what she was having to listen to.

Just before the class was due to finish, she gave in to her curiosity and reached down for them. As soon as she saw the heading – Leaflets of the White Rose – she forgot all about biology, and when she reached the request at the foot of the last page – *Please make as many copies of this leaflet as possible and pass them on!* – her heart was beating so hard it threatened to crack her ribs.

It is certainly the case today that every honest German is ashamed of his government. Sophie could have cheered. She was reading a slightly older, differently-worded leaflet from the one sent to the café-owner – and clearly it had passed through a lot of hands – but its message was similar:

Adopt non-violent resistance wherever you are, and stop this godless war before it is too late, before the last city is a heap of rubble, like Cologne, and before the youth of our nation bleeds to death on some battlefield because of the foolish pride of one sub-human.

The *Führer* called sub-human! *Ashamed! Resistance!* Every word Sophie read was music to her ears. As the class filed out, she shuffled the leaflet in among her own papers and slipped the whole lot into her satchel, then headed straight for Hans's lodgings.

'A stupid, pointless thing' – that's what her typically over-protective older brother had called the White Rose. Well, she didn't need protecting from this, and she needed to let him know.

All the way there, the leaflet seemed to burn a hole in her bag. She knew she'd be punished if she was caught with it – and she dreaded to think what might happen to the person who'd dared to write it, a person perhaps like Professor Huber. *He who does not act does not exist* came back to her with fresh force.

Hans wasn't home. Sophie remembered he had to

help run a clinic each week at this time, but it didn't last all day so she decided to hang on and wait.

There were worse places to pass an hour. Hans had turned the room into an art gallery with bright, light-filled posters of paintings by French artists, which the meat-headed Nazis would have called unpatriotic.

But even as she admired each image in turn, whenever she thought of the White Rose leaflet in her bag, Sophie trembled. Its words were imprinted on her mind. Even so, she finally sat down at Hans's cluttered desk to study them in more detail.

She hadn't quite remembered it all.

First time through, she'd skimmed most of the later text, largely made up of quotes by two great men from German history. The first was a writer called Friedrich Schiller, the second a favourite poet of Hans's, Johann Wolfgang von Goethe. After the sentence *Don't forget that people always get the government they deserve!* there was a long description by Schiller of the way the brutal Spartans used to rule over their people in Ancient Greece.

Reading this more closely, Sophie felt a prickling across her shoulders.

On this very desk during her birthday party, she'd seen an old book about the Spartans lying open. Now it lay stacked on top of a pile just beside her, a slip of paper sticking out as a bookmark.

She took down the book and looked inside.

In front of her was the exact same passage she'd just read in the leaflet, and Hans had underlined it. The book beneath it in the pile was entitled *The Awakening of Epimenides* – written by Johann Wolfgang von Goethe.

The weight seemed to go out of Sophie's body.

Either Hans had read the White Rose's call to resist the Nazis, then looked up the quotes in his books – or else he himself had typed the words of treason! And she believed she knew which it was.

Sophie flinched as she heard the street door open. Moments later, Hans appeared in the doorway, his black hair swept back from his broad forehead.

Brother and sister locked eyes across the room.

Wordlessly Sophie held up in one hand the White Rose leaflet, in the other Hans's book. Very slowly he blinked, then he came in.

'Oh, one of those White Rose things?' he said. 'I told you it was nonsense. Destroy it. You know it's a crime just to read it.'

'And how much more of a crime to write it?'

That stopped Hans in his tracks, right by the desk where Sophie sat. He looked down at her as if he might laugh. 'What?'

'You are the White Rose!' Sophie's voice quaked as she shook the leaflet at him. 'You are the one who wrote this. And you are out of your mind, Hans, because if you're caught you will be killed and the shock will probably kill our parents too, not to mention me!'

Hans's eyes glittered. 'White Rose?' he snorted. 'I'm just a doctor, a student. You're the one who's out of their mind!'

He crossed the room to slam the street window shut. Sophie set down both book and leaflet but continued to track Hans with her eyes, as one day a Nazi interrogator might.

'You can't put me off that way,' she said as he turned back to face her. 'It's you, isn't it?'

'It is *not* me!' Hans stormed. 'Now go away and get on with your studies and leave me to get on with mine!'

But Hans never got this angry, not with anyone. And even as he shouted, a cloud passed over his features; and although his eyes blazed he could not hold Sophie's gaze.

'Oh, Hans,' she half moaned. 'Oh, Hans, what have you done?'

For a long moment he stayed silent. Then he jammed his fingers into his hair.

'I planned to tell you nothing,' he said huskily. 'Then you could never be called my accomplice. It's still not too late. Forget we had this conversation. Turn a blind eye to the whole thing.'

Sophie rushed out of the chair and wrapped her arms around him. A different kind of sister might then have broken down in floods of tears. Not Sophie.

'I think you're so brave too,' she astonished Hans by saying. 'And I'm proud of you for writing what many must be thinking. But tell me you've made your point now, and there won't be any more leaflets.'

'He can't do that,' said a voice from just outside the room.

Sophie jumped back, and there in the dim open doorway stood not just one man in uniform but three. In her horror she saw only the uniforms, not the men – three soldiers who'd heard the whole conversation.

Then she recognized who they were: at the front stood Schurik, behind him Willi and Christel.

'Sophie, the four of us are working together,' Schurik continued grimly. 'This is about much more than our own safety. The darkness has gone on too long. If we don't light a torch, who will? The war has got to end. The Nazis must be overthrown.'

'But Hans was correct to say what he did,' added Willi, easing past Schurik and taking both Sophie's hands loosely in his own. 'You must forget this, Sophie. The fewer people in on it, the better. Even Traute doesn't know the full story.'

Christel followed him into the room and shut the door. 'Concentrate on your studies, dear Sophie,' he said with his kindly soft smile. 'Wipe this from your mind.'

Sophie slipped her hands out of Willi's. She took another step back.

Like a firing squad, the four young men stood shoulder to shoulder before her, each of them eyeing her narrowly.

Sophie lifted her gaze above their heads to one of the posters, so full of gorgeous sunlight falling on water. *Forget*, they were telling her. *Turn a blind eye*. Like those millions of Germans who looked the other way while Hitler's murder squads drove the world ever deeper into the darkness.

She nodded her head. 'You're right,' she said at last.

Schurik looked at her with enormous relief. 'So you'll pretend this never happened?'

'On the contrary,' Sophie replied, standing up straighter in her long woollen skirt and crisp white blouse. 'You have persuaded me how vital the White Rose is, and it sounds as if you could use another petal. I wish to join the group!'

THE NERVE CENTRE

The four young men argued with Sophie into the night, making it crystal clear that as a member of the White Rose she'd be dicing with death. But nothing they said would dissuade her, so at last each fell silent. Then, day by day, they brought her up to speed on the double lives they'd all been leading to run the campaign.

As Sophie discovered, it was pretty well-organized, and unbelievably risky.

Getting hold of a working typewriter in wartime was tricky enough, but that had been the easy part. Once Hans and Schurik worked out what to write in the leaflets, then typed them up, they had to be copied by the hundred. So, in a distant office-supplies shop, Schurik had managed to buy a second-hand duplicating machine ('at a first-hand price!' he joked). But where could all those copies be made without attracting snoopers?

This was where it got really interesting for Sophie.

One night, under cover of the blackout, Hans and Schurik escorted her to the garden of a smart house in Leopold Street. 'It belongs to an architect friend,' Hans told her as he unlocked the door to a spacious studio. 'He's often away in the east on government business,' added Schurik, 'but he detests the Nazis, so he lets us use this place for our work.'

He led the way down into a windowless cellar, and there on a bench was the hand-operated duplicator that looked like a fun-sized slot machine, with stacks of printed papers and envelopes.

Sophie ran her eyes over everything. So this is it, she thought: the nerve centre of the operation.

'We're running low on envelopes,' Schurik noted.

'All these wartime shortages,' Hans told Sophie with a sigh. 'Envelopes, paper, postage stamps. And we can't buy too many items all at once either, or shopkeepers will wonder what they're for.'

'Nor can we post too many envelopes in the same box!'

Hans picked up the top pages – a third White Rose leaflet which Sophie had read back at his lodgings, now ready to be mailed out. He folded one, sealed it in an envelope and passed it to her. The unstamped envelope had already been addressed, all the names and street numbers of possible supporters lifted from city directories. This raised a question in Sophie's mind.

'Do you keep a list of all the people you target?' she asked, passing the envelope back to Hans.

'Certainly not!' said Schurik. 'If the Gestapo ever got hold of something like that, they'd round up every person on it.'

'Then maybe you should say so in a leaflet?' Sophie suggested. 'That there's no list of contacts? Just to reassure them?'

Hans and Schurik exchanged a glance.

'Maybe we should,' said Schurik. 'Yes, maybe we should.'

Already Sophie was taking off her coat and drawing up a chair. 'I can stuff all these envelopes,' she said. 'And tomorrow I'll see where I can buy some more.'

'Perfect,' said Hans. 'Take whatever cash we've got. I'm not sure how much there is at the moment. Someone should really keep a record of all the money coming in and going out.' He caught Schurik's eye. 'Could you do that, Sophia?'

'With pleasure,' she replied as she set to work. 'So everything is funded by us, is that right?'

'Plus anyone we trust who wants to chip in,' said Schurik. 'We've had some really generous donations. Businessmen and so on.'

'That might be worth mentioning too?' said Sophie. 'To stop anyone thinking we're being funded by the countries we're fighting.'

Both men looked hard at her, then slowly began to nod. But Sophie saw Hans had something on his mind, and as they were leaving the cellar he turned to her and spelled it out:

'Sophia, it's still not too late for you to walk away.'

'Your parents would surely want you to,' added Schurik.

Sophie smiled. 'To exist I have to act,' she told them. 'This is my struggle too. I'll never walk away.'

Now leading a double life of her own, Sophie went on with her studies while throwing herself into the work of the group.

She didn't have the faintest doubt she was doing the right thing. As they cracked on with producing leaflet number four – *Every word that comes out of Hitler's mouth is a lie* was a line from it she especially liked – she realized she'd never felt more alive.

After saying her nightly prayers, she'd lie awake gazing at two sweetly-scented roses she had placed in a jar on her bedside table, marvelling at the strings of tiny water-beads on their leaves and stems. Regardless of who ran the world, nature's wonders lived on, and that gave Sophie hope, but it made her shiver too: trees and flowers didn't care how bestial humans could be.

One of her roses was pink, the other the colour of apricots. The group members had all given different answers when she'd asked why they had chosen the name 'White Rose'. Schurik's had pleased her the most: 'Because it stands for beauty and purity!'

Quite a lot about Hans's stylish Russian-born friend pleased Sophie. His family had left his mother's homeland when he was only four, he'd told her; now his fondest dream was to be a sculptor. And it was Schurik who dropped by one morning in late July to invite Sophie to a party at the studio.

'Oh, lovely!' she said. 'What's it a party for?'

'Hans, Willi and I are going to be taking a trip out east,' he said quite breezily, but as he spoke he lowered his eyes.

'Out east?' asked Sophie, a knot forming in her stomach.

Schurik's expression when he looked up became almost apologetic. 'We always knew it had to happen sometime.'

'You've had your marching orders?' said Sophie in a small hoarse voice. 'The Russian Front? Oh my God.'

Until the evening of the party, Sophie could hardly think straight. Unlike her brother Werner who was in combat on the eastern front, the boys wouldn't have to fight – they just had to tend to the wounded. Even so, they'd be in the most tremendous danger. They had all been fearing for her safety; now she was full of worry for them.

Yet their going-away party the night before they left was lively and high-spirited. All the guests knew and approved of the White Rose campaign, but only the hardest core knew who lay behind the leaflets. Now that things between Hans and Traute were cooling, Sophie spotted her brother paying lots of attention to a student friend of hers called Gisela. She also caught part of a chat between Hans and a man who looked a bit out of place in that youthful crowd: Professor Kurt Huber.

'These leaflets are all very well,' the Prof spluttered over his drink, unaware he was talking to their main author, 'though I don't agree with everything they say about Germany. But to save our Fatherland, more drastic action is required.'

Hans paused in spreading jam on some fruit cake. 'Such as?'

The old Prof had got himself very agitated. He twisted himself up closer to Hans to hiss in his ear, '*Assassination!*'

Catching her brother's eye, Sophie smartly moved off.

Her old feelings of utter helplessness were creeping up on her again – helplessness and deep frustration. For the next three to four months she wouldn't be able to oppose the Nazis in any way herself – the others had insisted all White Rose activity should be put on ice until their return. They simply wouldn't let Sophie keep things ticking over in their absence; she even wondered if their hearts would still be in the campaign after such a long break.

As the evening drew to a close, talk inevitably turned to what might await Hans, Willi and Schurik out east, where the Germans' supposedly invincible armies still hadn't captured the city of Stalingrad.

'Watch out for those diabolical Russians, won't you?' someone joked. 'According to Goebbels and co, they eat their own young!'

'Ah yes,' laughed Schurik. 'Back in the mother country, Mum was forever sinking her teeth into me!'

First thing next morning Sophie was there at Munich's East Station, wrapped up in her broad-stitched knitted jacket to see them off on their troop train. She dreaded to think it, but quite possibly this was the last time she would ever see her dear Hans.

'May God watch over you,' she whispered, embracing him before he boarded.

'May He watch over you too!' replied Hans, drawing her closer.

As Sophie watched the train pull out, the promise in the last words of the fourth and final White Rose leaflet helped to strengthen her spirit: *We will not be silent. We are your bad conscience. The White Rose will not leave you in peace!*

But now for months on end all Sophie could do was count down the days, and the wait turned out even bleaker than she'd imagined.

In order to be allowed to return to university in the autumn, she had to work in an arms factory during her vacation. Her father was briefly jailed too, his own secretary having reported him for cursing Hitler and saying the Russians were bound to overcome the German army. Then, as a result of all the extra stress this brought, Sophie's mother's health took a serious turn for the worse.

Bleakness upon bleakness: and through it all Sophie prayed as she had never prayed before for Hans to return alive from Russia. To lose him now – not just a beloved brother, but her fellow White Rose freedom fighter – would be just too cruel to bear.

FOUR MONTHS LATER

STRIKING AT THE HEART

Hans did return. So did the other two. Now for the first time since the summer, Sophie's brother called all five of them together in the architect's studio. Plainly he had something to announce, but he was taking a while to get around to it, and that made Sophie uneasy.

She got up from her chair and crossed the floor to refill her teacup, walking past some pictures which an artist friend from Ulm had been painting there. Before returning, she paused to look at the four men, each of whom looked seriously troubled.

Hans had sent lots of letters home from Russia, although army censors vetted every word, but in the short while since coming back he'd seemed to be censoring himself. 'We saw things beyond description,' was all he'd ever say to Sophie, even though they were now sharing lodgings in Franz Joseph Street. She'd also overheard Schurik tell Christel that after being back in his Russian motherland, he no longer felt German. In the face of all this, would the White Rose group now have the stomach to go on resisting? Sophie needed an answer. This tension was really churning her up.

Quietly Hans apologized for the chill in the studio's air: owing to fuel shortages the furnace hadn't been lit. But the others were hardly likely to complain. As Schurik and Willi well knew, back in Russia temperatures would now be plunging below zero. Then, just as quietly, Hans began to tell a story from his time out east.

'She was a slender, sick-looking young Jewish woman,' he said. 'Part of a female work group, she was swinging this huge pickaxe. I saw the agony in her face, saw too how attractive she must once have been. She obviously needed an iron supplement more than I did, so I took out my ration – the mixture of chocolate, dried fruit and nuts – and handed it to her. She threw it to the ground.'

Hans winced. Sophie wondered where this could be leading.

'I didn't blame her. She saw me as the enemy, another hated German in uniform. And why shouldn't she? But I picked up the food and dusted it down. I also picked a wild flower that was growing on the embankment, and I laid the ration and the flower at her feet.'

Hans blinked, struggling to keep his voice steady.

'Then I walked away, but when I looked back, the ration had been picked up, and the girl was wearing the flower in her hair.'

In the silence that followed, Sophie – still standing with her teacup – felt her hand flutter up to touch the slide she wore in her own hair. Hans was sounding so low, so resigned. Was he about to break the news that his heart was no longer in the White Rose?

He took a long deep breath. Then he went on with great emphasis: 'We need to prove to all decent people that not every German is an enemy. What we've done as a group so far has only scratched the surface. We now need to strike at the heart of the Nazi state.'

At last! Sophie's heart lifted. The fight would go on!

'"Strike"?' said Christel, not quite able to hide his alarm behind a smile. 'You're not suggesting we adopt the Prof's idea?'

'Assassinate the *Führer*?' asked Hans. 'No. That will never be our way. The White Rose's only weapon is the written word.'

'But there *have* been plots to assassinate him,' put in Schurik, pipe clamped between his teeth. 'The Nazis just kept them out of the news.'

Sophie blinked. Just imagining it gave her goose-bumps.

'I would like to bring the Prof on board, though,' Hans resumed. 'I want him to know we are the White Rose, and that he's welcome to contribute to our leaflets. His mind is quite brilliant. He'd make a far better case against the war than we can.'

Christel pursed his lips. 'Might the stakes not be too high for him? He has a wife, two young children. If our cover should be blown, the Nazis would execute him and make life hell for his family. Can we expect him to risk that?'

Christel's question hovered in the air. He could have been speaking about his own situation, although Christel's wife was now about to have a third child. He had always, understandably, been the most cautious of the plotters. The other men swapped glances.

'Let's approach the Prof,' said Willi. 'He can always say no.'

'Agreed,' said Hans. 'Now let's discuss the rest of the plan.'

It made Sophie dizzy to hear what Hans and Schurik then set out. They'd learned that all over Germany there were people, whole groups of them, lurking under the radar just like themselves. There were even plotters in the army, as well as cells of civilians in various towns and cities preparing to resist the Nazis.

The risks would be greater than ever, but for Hans, contacting them now had to be the White Rose's priority, so that their anti-war message could go nationwide. More helpers would be needed to set up a network, more money would have to be raised to pay for an expanded operation, but this – most surely – was the moment to strike. That sounded good to Sophie. Whatever it took, she'd throw herself in.

'The tide of the war in the east is turning,' Hans declared. 'It's not just that we haven't yet taken Stalingrad – the Russians are coming back at us in a counter-offensive!'

Sophie gasped. 'Then what Father got sent to prison for saying may turn out to be right?'

'In time, yes,' said Willi. 'But before that happens, we must persuade all true Germans to rise up and get rid of the Nazis.'

'Well said, Willi,' cried Schurik, clapping him on the back. 'Now lighten the mood please with one of your jokes.'

'Oh!' said Willi. He paused, then gave a grim smile. 'Have you heard that German dentists are now removing teeth through the nose? Why? Because no one dares to open their mouth any more!'

Everyone, including Christel, chuckled.

'And that's just what has to change,' said Hans, calling the meeting to a close. 'We've got to get people talking – then stop this accursed war before we lose it.'

THE WORST GERMAN EVER

After another long day at Gestapo HQ, Robert Mohr was heading for the exit when his head of department, a man by the name of Schäfer, happened to fall into step alongside him.

Mohr returned his greeting warily: few encounters in this place were genuinely random. As they walked on together to the end of the long corridor, Mohr soon learned what was on his mind.

'That spate of leaflets last summer – it dried up?'

'That is our understanding, sir. A few more have been handed in since, but all were copies of the same original four leaflets.'

'What was it the traitors called themselves? White Heart?'

'White Rose, sir.'

'And we believe it was a purely local operation?'

'Again, sir, that is our understanding. Analysis suggests the paper and envelopes they used were all sourced within this area.'

Schäfer narrowed his eyes at the approaching doorway. 'So four treasonable leaflets appeared, all from the same unknown hand, over a period of eight or nine weeks – then nothing?'

'Perhaps, sir,' suggested Mohr, 'whoever was behind them saw the error of their ways?'

Schäfer shot Mohr a sidelong glance. 'We must hope you are right. You're aware that those leaflets were regarded as hostile to the state in the highest degree?'

'Indeed, sir. But they failed to provoke any kind of revolt.'

Schäfer nodded, peering out at the descending night. 'We must hope too there are no more fireworks tonight.' He indicated the skies from which Allied bombers had steadily been pulverizing their city. 'I believe you have a son fighting for the *Führer* against the barbarous Russians. Doubtless in his letters home he has told you total victory for the Fatherland is imminent?'

Mohr met his gaze. He'd trained himself to block out thoughts of his son at the Front, but still it was hard not to be anxious.

'Victory, as you say, sir, cannot be far away.'

* * *

Schäfer's hopes were dashed: again that night, bombs rained down on Munich. But while he was taking shelter, Mohr replayed the conversation in his mind, and worked out why the subject of those leaflets had come up again. Having read between the lines of his son's letters, he suspected that victory in the east was as distant as ever. Mohr's Nazi masters were surely now afraid that if more leaflets appeared, they might find more willing readers, and even encourage resistance at home.

There could, of course, be no question of letting that happen. First thing next morning he'd brief his staff on the need to step up their vigilance. There were one or two leads from the summer he would follow up himself as well. Neither he nor Schäfer could truly rest until they had flushed out the criminal organization involved.

One week later, on a rare bomb-free evening, Sophie accompanied Hans along the blacked-out streets into Munich city centre.

All the stores had long since closed, but the door to a bookshop on Maximiliansplatz had been left ajar. Hans ushered Sophie in ahead of him. No forbidden electric lights burned inside, just a handful of candles flickering far to the rear. They faintly illuminated a circle of ten or so young people: the expanded core of the White Rose group, complete with its new and trusted helpers.

Hans was greeted by the shop's much older owner, Josef Sönghen, standing behind the counter to cash up his day's takings. 'The fearless Sophie too!' he said fondly. 'Do go through for your meeting, please. You won't be disturbed.'

'You're sure it's safe to talk here?' hissed one of the girls, almost before Hans and Sophie took their seats.

'As safe as anywhere,' grinned Hans.

'Josef Sönghen is a really valuable supporter,' Sophie assured the girl. 'He's even agreed that if the authorities start sniffing around the studio, he'll store our printing equipment here.'

Swiftly they got down to the evening's main business: reporting back on the solid progress some of them had been making in the regions, forging links with other anti-Nazi cells.

Person after person described how the security presence on the streets and on public transport seemed much more obvious. As if to underline this point, back at the counter Josef coughed loudly and dropped a heavy book to the floor – a pre-arranged alarm signal.

Moments later, a man stepped into the shop, removing his hat.

Everyone froze as he scanned the dim interior before he flashed his ID at Josef. Giving his name as Robert Mohr, he hardly needed to go on and specify which organization he belonged to.

Gestapo.

A boy near to Sophie groaned under his breath. But Josef wasn't fazed. 'I am so sorry, sir,' he cried. 'This shop is closed!'

The agent stepped further inside. 'But your door is open,' he said. 'I have watched others come in.' He nodded towards the shop's murky depths where he must have been able to see silhouettes.

'Ah, we are holding a small discussion this evening. This past year, we have held a number. For university students, you see?'

Still hardly daring to breathe, Sophie watched the overcoated agent study the book spines on the nearest shelves, doubtless on the lookout for banned works. 'What will you be discussing this evening?' he asked Josef, turning.

'Tonight? Ah, new work from the regions, sir. Publications which emphasize the excellence of all corners of Germany!' He held up for inspection the large volume that had clattered to the floor earlier. As Josef well knew, this was a category of literature actively promoted by the Ministry of Propaganda and Enlightenment which had to approve every new book that was published.

Still, however, the agent lingered.

'You have only one copy of our *Führer*'s book,' he pointed out, referring to *My Struggle*, in which Hitler gave his own life story alongside his vision for

Germany's future; one White Rose leaflet said it was *written in the worst German I have ever read*.

Josef pulled an offended face. 'Only today, sir, I ordered more. The great book sells so fast we cannot keep up with demand!'

When at last the agent could find no further reason to stay, Josef bade him farewell, then waited behind his counter for a full minute before crossing to the door and locking it. The night really did seem to have swallowed the Gestapo man up.

'"The excellence of all corners of Germany"!' repeated Willi, setting off a ripple of jittery laughter when Josef went through to confirm that the coast was clear. 'Well, that wasn't a total lie!'

Sophie noticed how seriously disturbed some of the others were looking. To get things straight back on track, she tapped her brother on the knee. 'Hans,' she said, 'why don't you tell everyone about the new leaflet we're putting together?'

'Leaflet five!' Hans responded eagerly. 'Yes indeed, a few of us are pitching in on this one' – he tilted his head back at Sophie, which caused her to blush – 'including, we very much hope, a certain professor you will all be familiar with—'

'Prof Huber?' someone cried out in disbelief.

'You've told him and he's in, Hans?' asked the watching Josef.

'I have revealed to him that we're the White Rose,

yes. But no, we're still trying to persuade him to join us. Geniuses like him don't find it all that easy to pitch in with anyone! But even without the Prof, this new leaflet is a really big step in a new direction.'

Sophie watched the others' faces as Hans went on to describe in detail what he meant. For a start, leaflet five didn't have a 'White Rose' caption at the top. Instead it was headed, *LEAFLETS OF THE RESISTANCE MOVEMENT IN GERMANY*, then the text began with *A Call to All Germans!* For another thing, it was much shorter than the others – and without any complicated quotes from long-dead writers! Readers of the earlier leaflets had told Hans to get to the point quicker. What people really wanted to know, they said, was what sort of new Germany might be built if the Nazis were removed.

So leaflet five described a land where everyone would be able to speak, write, live and worship freely, where workers would not be virtual slaves, and all this would be based on *generous, open cooperation* between *all* the peoples of Europe.

'And who in their right minds could disagree with all that?' sighed Christel. 'But are there really enough people out there to make up a *national* resistance movement? Are we right to believe others are now seeing things the same way we do?'

Several others voiced their own doubts. Sophie wasn't one of them, but every now and then even she had to wonder about these things. Hans did sometimes let his sheer enthusiasm get the better of him. He looked around the circle with a gleam in his eye.

'Oh, they're out there, you'll see!' he said. 'They're right on the point of revolt. I tell you, the stone is beginning to roll!'

9

UPROAR AT THE MUSEUM

Munich's German Museum was packed to the rafters with college staff and students. To celebrate the university's founding 470 years earlier, a speech was due to be given by one of the region's top Nazi officials, but although every student had been ordered to attend, the core White Rose group was staying away.

Traute, however, went along with a few of the group's outer circle, and when she reported back on what happened next, it seemed – to Sophie's immense delight – that Hans had been right to feel so confident: the stone really was beginning to roll.

Balding, beaky-nosed Paul Giesler clearly wore his Nazi uniform with great pride over his pot belly; and soon it was clear he loved the sound of his own voice too. The trouble was, very few others in the vast building liked what he was saying. In fact, they could hardly believe their ears.

Instead of praising the university for nearly five centuries of fine scholarship, he complained that too many current students were dodging their responsibility to the Fatherland, so they should be drafted at once into the army, or put to work in the arms factories.

'What kind of young man hides his nose in a book when he could be winning glory on the battlefield!' Giesler sneered.

There was a murmur of distaste among the uniformed student-soldiers seated at ground level – some of them wounded men with canes and crutches. Faculty members in their academic robes, including Kurt Huber, also shifted restlessly on their chairs.

Giesler then turned his anger and ridicule on the female students, most of whom were listening from the balcony:

'As for you healthy-bodied young women, you should be making more valuable contributions of your own – like producing a child every year for the Fatherland, preferably a boy child!'

At that, there were louder murmurs, and some scraping of shoe soles against the floor, which was a way of booing with your feet. Giesler didn't understand that. He thought his crude language was amusing the audience, so he made it even cruder.

'Of course,' he went on with a smirk, 'you can't make babies on your own. But if any of you girls haven't yet been able to attract a mate, I'd be glad to let officers from my staff be the fathers, every one of them men of the purest German blood—'

At that point the first women in the balcony walked out. Whistles filled the air, then shouts of outrage. Giesler's voice could no longer be heard, and that's when the real mayhem began.

Male students got up to leave too, only for SS guards posted in the doorways to restrain them. Scuffles started, punches were thrown. Then when the guards made dozens of arrests, waves of new students joined the protest and forced their way outside.

It didn't end there. Hordes of the young men and women linked arms and marched off down Ludwig Street. 'Free our comrades!' they chanted at the tops of their voices. 'Give us back our comrades!'

Everyone who saw it was amazed. No such demonstration had ever taken place on the streets of Nazi Germany. More amazingly still, no one had organized it in advance. The students looked jubilant, as if they were relieved to be standing up for common decency at last.

There was no telling what might have happened next if Giesler hadn't shown just how focused the

Nazis were on eliminating any kind of opposition. Screams filled the air as he sent in droves of baton-wielding riot police who lashed out with appalling brutality – and the marching columns were broken up.

Back at Franz Joseph Street, Traute told the whole stunning tale to Sophie, Hans and the others. Similar breathless conversations took place all over the city. The Nazis were able to stop the protest from being mentioned in the press, but news still got around by word of mouth into parts of Germany far beyond Munich.

Sophie saw a steely boyish satisfaction in Hans's eyes all that week. It was as if his favourite sports team had gone on a winning streak and looked like topping the league!

With reports of Nazi victories on foreign fields now drying up, suddenly it seemed that people like themselves had everything to play for. The Prof thought so too. Impatient at his fellow staff members for just putting up with Giesler's vile speech, he got word to the White Rose that he was ready to discuss ways to help them.

'Maybe our leaflets played a part in this protest,' Hans told the group. 'Many of those marchers will have read them and come to see our idea is right. I've told you people like us exist all over Germany.

Together, if we act fast, we *can* force an end to this war.'

Everyone but Christel nodded. His wife was about to give birth, but Sophie understood this wasn't his sole cause for concern.

'We mustn't get carried away,' he warned. 'The Nazis will be on red alert for any kind of "disloyalty" now. One false step,' he dragged a finger across his throat, 'and we're dead.'

Sophie swallowed hard.

She understood why Christel might want to take things slower, but she saw it more Hans's way: the time for holding back had surely passed. Once a big stone starts to roll, it's so hard to stop it.

NIGHT MISSION

It was late, it was dark, it was cold, and Sophie didn't think she had ever felt so tense. She couldn't forget Christel dragging his finger across his throat. Had the White Rose's gentlest soul been right to advise more caution?

Heart in mouth, she lugged her heavy rucksack on board yet another train out of Munich, wondering if Hans or Schurik or Willi felt the same way when they set off on their own missions to even more distant destinations.

At least Sophie only had to transport her cargo of leaflets within the quite local area of Augsburg, Ulm, where she came from, and her target city for tonight, Stuttgart. If they'd been able to travel in pairs, that might have helped. But they all knew they couldn't take the risk of two of them being captured together; and from each mission's start to its end, capture was a constant possibility.

Sophie loaded the rucksack onto the overhead rack in the first compartment she entered. Then, praying none of the other passengers was watching too closely, she found a seat for herself several compartments down the long narrow corridor.

Danger was everywhere: military policemen on patrol, the man in the next seat who could be Gestapo… They mightn't have been deliberately looking out for someone like her – their main targets were deserters from the armed forces or food-smugglers in this increasingly hungry country – but to them, everyone was fair game.

Sophie knew what to do next. Sit calmly; draw no attention, even during long delays while bomb-damaged track was being repaired; keep her papers ready for checking. Even more crucially, she kept mentally rehearsing her excuse if anyone should ask her why she was on the train at all: an emergency trip back to Ulm to look after a sick relative. If she was caught as far away as Stuttgart, then she'd say that in her rush she'd caught the wrong train. Apart from anything else, it was exhausting to have to keep thinking so hard.

But it was worth it. All this was so worth it.

* * *

The journey seemed to take for ever.

Then at last Sophie was able to go back for her rucksack and step out into the deep midwinter.

Her breath made clouds in the cold night air as she picked her way around the rubble outside the station. Then she headed into the dark streets with her latest load, searching for public mailboxes to post her leaflets batch by batch without being spotted.

Support the resistance was the final rallying cry of the explosive fifth leaflet inside all her envelopes. *Distribute the leaflets!* To make the stone roll faster still, this one was not just being sent to all points in the German-speaking world. It was being sent *from* them too. Sophie's batches of leaflets would now head off to their destinations bearing postmarks from Ulm and Stuttgart. Her comrades were posting leaflets in other towns and cities. That way, the authorities would assume a nationwide network already existed, and that was why, night after night at the studio, the core White Rose group had cranked out masses more copies than usual of leaflet five. Thousands now, not just hundreds.

On nights like this Sophie felt she was lugging millions of the things around on her back. Yet she couldn't afford to let any passing policeman spot how heavy her load was. Having to concentrate on that at least stopped her dwelling on the fear she felt. But as she zigzagged from mailbox to mailbox, she couldn't keep all her negative thoughts at bay.

Es gibt für uns nur

Many of these centred on the Prof. He really hadn't fitted into the team very smoothly – starting to argue almost at once about the leaflet's wording. When he came to the Scholls' lodgings he'd ranted in particular at Schurik for his 'pro-Russian' input, and as he made furiously clear, he believed only the German army would ever be able to overthrow Hitler, not a people's uprising.

Hans and Schurik – with a little help from Sophie – had got their way this time. But the quarrels left a sour taste, and with Christel also constantly advising caution, Sophie sensed more problems up ahead in keeping the team united.

After a couple of hours, rucksack emptied, Sophie returned in deep relief to the station, papers and excuses at the ready. And this time she really did take the chance to travel back to Ulm to see how her parents were doing.

Next morning, as she packed some bits of food her mother had set aside for her and Hans, she found her bag was not in fact quite empty. She pulled out a single scrunched-up loose leaflet, and her eyes fell on a sentence that never failed to stir her: *Every nation and each man has a right to the goods of the whole world!*

'What have you got there?' barked her father, who'd come back into the kitchen without Sophie noticing.

She put on her most innocent expression. 'Oh, just something I found in Munich.'

She began to stuff it back in the bag but her father, a large stern man in shirtsleeves and braces, held out his hand.

'Show me.'

There was no way Sophie could avoid handing the leaflet over.

Her father put on his glasses and read the whole thing where he stood, then passed it back with a sniff.

'Brave words,' he told her. 'Very brave and very true – whoever wrote them.' He paused. 'You found it, you say?'

'Yes, Father. At the university.'

She met his eye and his face darkened. 'I sincerely hope you and Hans aren't involved?'

'Us? How could you possibly think so! Whatever goes on around us in Munich, I assure you Hans and I always keep our noses clean.'

His gaze stayed on her until finally he nodded.

'You've always been the wisest of my women,' he said. 'But destroy that thing before you leave this house. If your bag is inspected and they find it, they'd show you absolutely no mercy.'

INTO AN ABYSS

As soon as Robert Mohr arrived at Gestapo HQ that January morning a call came through from his head of department's secretary. Mohr was to drop everything and come to Schäfer's office at once.

As Mohr paced down the corridor, his tread was a little heavy. For Munich citizens like him the war had been a distant affair until recently. Now they were not just being targeted by Allied bombers at night, each day they saw more and more bewildered-looking refugees fetching up on Munich's streets after their homes had been destroyed in the Fatherland's industrial north. The longer this went on, the lower morale would sink, especially as some shocking rumours had begun to circulate in place of hard news from Stalingrad; Mohr had to re-double his efforts not to fret about his own son's safety.

He knocked on the door and entered.

Talking on the phone, Schäfer didn't look at him, his gaze fixed instead on the *Führer*'s framed portrait on the office's far wall. His free hand rested on a pile of creased paper sheets.

Waiting at attention for what felt like a short eternity, Mohr put two and two together. Those papers had to be more leaflets. The nameless rebel writers must have struck again. Schäfer had never liked loose ends: now his concern that the White Rose group was still at large seemed justified.

He put down his phone and trained his eyes on Mohr. 'You were wrong about our enemies within,' he said, raising his palm then slapping it down on the papers. 'They have not seen the error of their ways.'

He grabbed a leaflet and thrust it up at Mohr, who read it quickly with no expression on his face, but his blood ran cold:

It has become a mathematical certainty that Hitler is leading the German people into an abyss... A criminal regime cannot achieve a German victory. Separate yourselves before it is too late *from everything connected with National Socialism. Afterwards, a terrible but just judgement will be handed out to those who stayed in hiding, who were cowardly and hesitant.*

'That leaflet,' Schäfer said steadily when Mohr handed it back, 'surfaced not here but in Berlin. Another appeared in Augsburg, but it had a Stuttgart postmark. While these,' again he slapped the pile of papers, 'are turning up all over this city – in mailboxes, parked cars, telephone kiosks, scattered in doorways and halls, on park benches. The filth is everywhere, and they're still being handed in by the hundred. It could in the end be thousands.'

Mohr lifted his chin, caught in a kind of crossfire between Shäfer's gaze and that of the *Führer* in the portrait behind him. But since he hadn't yet been invited to speak, he said nothing.

Now at last Schäfer's voice began to tremble. 'This is causing,' he said, 'the greatest disturbance and dismay at the highest levels of the party and the state in Berlin.'

Mohr's mouth tightened. He didn't need those men in Germany's capital city to be named. Schäfer meant Heinrich Himmler, head of all the country's security forces; maybe even the man in the portrait whose gaze continued to bore into the back of Mohr's head.

'It cannot go on,' Schäfer declared. 'This plot began here and here it must end. We are dealing with significant enemies of the people. Berlin requires us to find them and make an example of them. An example which no one will be able to forget.'

His eyes narrowed.

'As of now, you will set aside all your other work and put together a special task force to remove this threat. Is that clear?'

Mohr stood straighter and pushed out his chest. He got the message: maybe more than just his job was on the line now.

'Sir,' he replied, 'very clear.'

If Mohr's step had been heavy on his way to Schäfer's office, by that week's end he felt lead weights had been attached to both feet.

Schäfer had not overestimated the leaflets' numbers. As Mohr's Gestapo colleagues in other cities soon corroborated, there really were thousands of the things, and they were being sent from many cities, including Ulm, Frankfurt and Vienna.

THE RESISTANCE MOVEMENT IN GERMANY, they were now calling themselves: truly it seemed to be a nationwide operation, but a gut feeling still told Mohr the true enemy lay closer to home. Again he was having the leaflets' paper and envelopes analysed to track down their sources. Experts were also at work examining the leaflets' text, to provide a profile of the kind of person or people who'd written them. Yet if the traitors were operating out of Munich, their leaflets would somehow need to be distributed from there. So Mohr had ordered closer watches for any suspicious activity on the rail and road networks, including even lone travellers with heavy baggage.

Mohr knew how high the stakes now were. Support from the public was vital to the war effort. He recalled Minister Goebbels spelling out just how vital: *When a German soldier turns his face to the enemy*, he'd told the nation, *he can be absolutely confident that the home front stands solidly behind him*. But could that soldier really be so confident? Could Robert Mohr's son at the Front still take such support for granted?

Then something happened. Something Mohr had been dreading. Something that might make ordinary Germans more receptive still to the leaflets' message – and which made it even more urgent for his Gestapo team to run the group to ground and wipe it out:

On 3rd February a news bulletin interrupted regular German radio programming. First there was a roll of drums, quite a muffled sound, followed by silence. The drum roll came again. A momentous announcement was about to be made, but usually at these times there were triumphant fanfares.

A piece of music followed, written by Ludwig van Beethoven, the mighty German composer.

The Battle of Stalingrad has ended, came the news at last. *The Sixth German Army under the inspirational leadership of Field Marshal von Paulus has been overcome by the enemy...*

Almost unthinkably, the Fatherland had suffered defeat!

Over 200,000 German soldiers had perished; 90,000 more were being marched by the Russians through the snows to Siberian prison camps. For three days of national mourning, concert halls, cinemas and theatres would be shut. The back pages of newspapers, bordered in black, would fill up with so many Iron Crosses in memory of fallen soldiers that they would look like little cemeteries.

They died so Germany may live, the radio bulletin proclaimed. Mohr, whose son mercifully had survived, could only hope this turned out to be true. So too, in a different part of Munich, and for very different reasons, did Sophie Scholl when the news came through to her.

Here was the catastrophic disaster she and her group had been predicting for months. Surely now Germans everywhere would see the war could not be won, that the sacrifice of lives must end?

Yet Hans seemed oddly preoccupied when she ran into him hurrying off the university campus later that day with Schurik and Willi. The three of them could so easily have ended up as little Iron Crosses in the newspaper – but though they greeted Sophie warmly, it was clear they weren't in a mood to celebrate quite yet.

'So where are you all heading?' she asked.

'Hans wants us to leave a mark of our own on this hugely significant day,' Willi began, sounding none too convinced himself, before Hans hurried him on with a slightly manic wink at Sophie.

'Prepare for a surprise!' he called back to her. 'While the iron is still hot, we have to strike!'

Then they were gone.

SOUL OF THE WHITE ROSE

On 4th February 1943, the sun rose on a rather different Munich from the city it had set on hours before.

Its buildings had been spared another pummelling from Allied bombers, but still there was the most unholy mess. At more than two dozen points around the city's central districts, the walls of apartment houses and state buildings had been stencilled with slogans in black tar-based paint.

The graffiti astounded crowds of Munich's early birds: *DOWN WITH HITLER!* in three-foot-high lettering. *FREEDOM!* There were even crossed-out swastikas.

As soon as word of this new treason reached the authorities, teams of cleaners were sent out to scrub away all traces. A furious Robert Mohr could be seen supervising one of them as they battled to remove slogans from the university's walls.

Almost incredibly to Mohr, not one citizen or night patrol had witnessed any of these enemies of the people at work. Possibly the same enemies who had produced the leaflets? Perhaps at this very university, or even in the shop of a sympathetic bookseller?

Whatever leads he might now follow, it chilled him that these 'artists' could strike at the city's heart then simply waltz away. And that, without Mohr having a clue about their identities, was exactly what Hans, Schurik and Willi had done: hauling their pots, brushes and stencils around the streets, one standing guard at each location with a loaded pistol while the others lashed on the paint.

Sophie, meanwhile, had a good idea what Hans had been up to when he hadn't come home the night before. She'd seen good-quality paint and brushes in the studio cellar, and Schurik had recently asked the painter at work there to show him how to create stencils.

On this of all days it had been a crazily brave gesture to make, but Sophie couldn't help wishing she'd been with them. All the boys tended to over-protect her now – happy to let her keep the group's accounts, or tell her no one was better at typing addresses on envelopes, yet shielding her from the most acute danger.

The three boys were still flushed from their escapade when they got together with Sophie at the studio. They even brought some wine to toast their success. On another rare visit from his posting at Innsbruck, Christel was able to be there too.

Hans was especially keyed-up. Earlier, he'd walked into the university past one of the slogans which no amount of scrubbing was ever going to remove. 'They'd covered it with great sheets of butcher's paper,' he laughed. 'But the paint was already showing through! A guy in my class came up, grinning all over his face, and he whispered, "Did you see it, Hans? Did you *see* it?"'

'And how did you reply?' Christel said severely.

'How do you think I replied? "See what?" I asked, then I walked on.' He shrugged. 'You don't seem pleased, Christel?'

Christel rose from his chair and crossed to the window. Automatically he checked that no one suspicious was lurking outside. Thanks first to the protest at the Museum, then the rash of new leaflets across the city, everyone knew the surveillance operation on Munich students had been stepped up.

'I think your action was reckless and unnecessary,' he said. 'Especially now. It's almost as if you want to be caught.'

Hans grinned. 'But now is exactly when this sort of action is needed! Now that the tide of war has turned.' He paused, and Sophie noticed with a pang how strung-out he looked, even a little pop-eyed. 'I'm planning to go back out with the brushes!'

'But don't you see?' Christel argued back. 'Starting to lose the war will only make them crack down harder. Already there are stories of people being executed just for saying we won't win.' He glanced at Sophie, hesitated, then went on anyway. 'And haven't you just had a tip-off, Hans, that the Gestapo's on your trail?'

Hans chose not to answer the last question. He smiled oddly at Christel. 'So you think we're being reckless?'

'If you risk drawing attention to the group like this, yes. Reckless, careless. And it's not just me. The Prof thinks so too.'

'Oh, really? Well, he's also just agreed to write leaflet six. The great Kurt Huber!'

Hans glanced around the room but the tension didn't lift, and both Schurik and Willi were keeping ominously quiet.

'Meanwhile,' Hans went on slightly too loudly, draining his wine glass and pouring a refill, 'a contact from the main resistance cell in Berlin will soon be coming to us here for talks.'

Abruptly then his mood altered. Sophie saw this happen more and more: the strain of running their campaign on top of all his studies had to be telling on him, not to mention being haunted by whatever atrocities he'd seen on the Eastern Front. He went across to Christel and slipped a friendly arm around his shoulder.

'We know you've got a lot to lose,' he said. 'So much more than the rest of us. The best thing you can do over at Innsbruck is draft a seventh leaflet, to follow straight on from the Prof's.'

At last the other two stirred, murmuring their agreement.

'Well, yes,' Christel conceded. 'Yes, I could do that.'

'Splendid!' cried Hans, refreshing all the glasses. 'You'll do it wonderfully. Say how we need a new United States of Europe under the protection of the US President once we've got rid of the Nazis!'

Christel nodded, but for some time Willi had been frowning at Sophie, who hadn't said a word since the conversation began.

'You look terribly solemn, Sophie,' he said. 'Would you care to hear one of my jokes?'

'Ha!' she smiled. 'No thanks, Willi. But there is one thing, Hans.'

'Say it, Sophia.'

'If you go out on another graffiti mission, can I come too?'

Back at their apartment, Sophie busied herself packing a suitcase. Their mother and one of their sisters had fallen ill, so their father had asked her to come home for a week or so to help around the house. She didn't mind going, but part of her felt that the one who might really need looking after was Hans.

'Reckless', Christel had called him, 'careless'. Was that the right way to read Hans's recent behaviour? On the other hand, did ever-bigger risks just have to be taken now? Sophie lay on her bed trying to work out her own answers, with a favourite gramophone record, the *Trout* quintet by Schubert, playing beside her.

When its sprightly fourth movement began, Hans came and leaned in obvious fatigue against her door-frame to listen with her.

'I so love that piece,' sighed Sophie when it was over. 'It conjures up for me – oh, springtime clouds in the sky! Budding branches stirred by the wind in bright young sunlight!' Despite the phenomenal pressures they were living under, she grinned and shook her head. 'Ah, I'm so looking forward to the spring!'

A wintry cloud passed over Hans's film-star features. Sophie guessed what he was about to say – that if the Gestapo really was on their trail, then perhaps none of them would live to see another spring. So she headed him off by making herself sound even cheerier.

As group leader, Hans had been getting too much criticism. Now that she'd thought it all over, Sophie decided he needed support.

'You know what Christel said about wanting to be caught?' she began. 'Well, sometimes I almost do want that! Just for me. Oh, and if ever I was caught, of course I'd never betray you others.'

This had always been a key part of the group's planning: if accused, first deny everything; then if proven guilty, shoulder the whole of the blame. But Hans's face was a picture of puzzlement.

'Just what are you driving at, little sister?' he asked.

Sophie blushed. 'Maybe we actually need to be *more* reckless, not less, and *really* draw attention to ourselves. First the leaflets, then the graffiti, and then – oh, Hans! – we could do something truly sensational, even if we're made to pay for it.' She paused. 'After all, so many people have had to die *for* the Nazis, why shouldn't we die opposing them? As Mother used to tell us, everyone's life on earth is just a doorway to eternity anyway.'

Hans gave her a searching look. 'Sophia,' he said, his tired face breaking into a smile, 'I do believe you've become the soul of the White Rose.'

'But you understand what I'm saying, Hans?'

He gave a firm nod. 'When you get back from Ulm, let's see how you and I can really stir things up. Now go to sleep,' he said, switching off the gramophone, then the light, 'and dream sweet dreams of the spring.'

TWO WEEKS LATER

SOMETHING TRULY SENSATIONAL

Day was yet to break on Thursday 18th February when Robert Mohr got to his desk. But the earlier he travelled in to work, the further he seemed to travel away from solving the riddle of the five leaflets. And now, to deepen the nightmare, a sixth lay in front of him.

The day of reckoning has come! it declared, its fiery message all but scorching the paper. *Freedom and honour: for ten long years Hitler and his comrades have squeezed, debased and twisted those beautiful words to the point of nausea…*

Leaflet six was popping up all over the city. A copy had even been mailed to Munich's chief of police! Mohr, like a mouse being played with by a cat, eyed it with loathing.

Not one of the local suspects chased down by his team had turned out to be behind this infernal business. Despite his offer of a large reward to anyone who could identify the smear campaigners, no one had come forward. Close to his wits' end, Mohr reached for a cigarette – his fifth already that morning. This had to be an operation of the highest sophistication, run by seasoned activists, men who were perhaps not even based in Munich at all.

Beresina and Stalingrad go up in flames in the East, and the dead of Stalingrad implore us to take action, he read with incredulity. *Up, up, my people, let smoke and flame be our sign!*

'Damn you, damn you, damn you!' Mohr spat at the sheet of paper, crunching it up in his fist and hurling it across the room.

This was not just another Thursday morning for Sophie Scholl.

Normally she took a class at 8.00 a.m. but today that class was well underway before she even got up. Hans rose just as late. Since her return from Ulm, they'd been putting in regular night shifts cranking out thousands of copies of the Prof's new leaflet, so they had to catch up on their sleep. Yet still Sophie felt drained, while Hans looked a pale copy of his old boisterous self.

The siblings ate their breakfast without saying much, Hans checking Christel's handwritten draft of leaflet seven, which he planned to type up later. Over by the main door stood the suitcase Sophie had unpacked just days earlier. Now it had been packed again, as had the smaller satchel leaning against it.

The weather had been bad recently, but strong sunlight streamed in through the windows: it seemed more like spring than the depths of winter. This really wasn't just another Thursday morning.

Around 10.30 a.m. the pair stood up and put on their overcoats. However bright it looked outside, there was still old snow on the ground and it wouldn't be warm. They looked each other in the eye.

Ready? Ready. 'Something truly sensational', Sophie had suggested two weeks earlier to her brother. This, now, would be it.

Hans picked up the case, Sophie the satchel. The university's main entrance was a ten-minute walk away. Ten minutes to hold their nerve before carrying out their most hazardous mission of all.

As they walked, Sophie's head teemed with all that had happened in the last fortnight.

Not altogether unexpectedly, the group had now shrunk to little more than just the two of them. Christel's draft for leaflet seven was really only a parting gesture. Over in distant Innsbruck, with a third child now in his care and a wife who'd fallen ill after the birth, he simply wasn't prepared to take yet more risks.

Schurik too had had enough. Instead of joining them today, the boy who no longer felt German had finally decided he had no place in Germany. His plan now was to escape, back to Mother Russia where his heart lay.

Walking on at Hans's side, Sophie plunged her free hand into her coat pocket and to her dismay she found the key to the studio, still there from the previous night's printing. This would be so dangerous if they were caught and searched, but fatigue could make you careless, to use Christel's word. Fatigue and constant tension.

A lot of that tension had been caused once again by Prof Huber. He'd written a fabulous leaflet six, but further disputes had arisen over the wording. The older man – still believing only soldiers could put an end to Nazism – had described the German army as *glorious*. Hans would not allow that, so the Prof had made a simple response: he'd cut all his ties with the group.

As she entered the university grounds with her brother, Sophie wondered if it was always this way with rebel bands: against the dark night of injustice could they flare brightly but only briefly?

Passing the tall, sun-kissed fountain in the square, Hans switched the case from one hand to the other.

Then they strode up the steps to the great silent inner courtyard, empty of people but flooded with light mainly through its high glass-domed roof.

It was still not long past 10.45, so all that morning's ten o'clock classes would still be in session. To accomplish their mission, this was just how Hans and Sophie needed it to be.

But then there was an unexpected hitch.

Who should they see skipping down the steps towards them but Willi and Traute. Sophie guessed at once they had left a class early and were heading for another lecture at the medical campus a short streetcar ride away. But when their friends saw Hans carrying the suitcase, their smiles of greeting faltered.

'Will you be coming to the lecture too?' Willi asked as he passed, now glaring at the case.

'No no, you go on,' was all Hans replied, barely breaking step.

Sophie glanced up at Hans; he shook his head. Traute had no idea what they were about to do. Willi may have known; he may even have tried to talk Hans out of it. All Sophie knew for sure was that she and Hans were on their own path now, and the quicker they got on with things before the packed lecture halls turned out, the better.

What happened next went like a dream. It was also quite easily the most hair-raising few minutes of Sophie's life.

Fellow students! leaflet six began – and how better to reach those students than by personally leafleting the university in broad daylight? Hans and Sophie opened the satchel and case and there they lay waiting: the better part of 2,000 copies.

Sophie's stomach lurched. They really were going to do this.

Hans glanced at his watch. 'Let's go,' he breathed.

Moving fast and lightly on their feet, they took one stack of pages after another and deposited them all round the building: on window sills, by the two large robed statues at the foot of the staircase, outside the wide wooden doors to the lecture halls, then up to the second-floor gallery with another row of doorways, the third floor with yet another. Stack after stack after stack.

At one point Sophie thought she might just seize up as they raced against time. But though she was racked by nerves, she had joined the White Rose in order to exist and this, truly, was existing. Whatever the others thought, she knew Hans had been right: now was the moment to send out the loudest-ever *no* to the Nazis.

Up in the third-floor gallery they grabbed the last two stacks of leaflets and balanced them on the marble balcony wall before refastening their bags. The clock behind them showed that it was about to strike eleven, when all the doors below would open, all the students would emerge, then all those laid-out leaflets would be picked up and read. *Up, up, my people!*

But their work was still not quite done.

To signal the end of the classes a bell rang, and all around the building doors swung open. Sophie glanced up at her brave and brilliant brother. It felt like only yesterday that they had played together as carefree children in the woods and fields around Ulm.

Hans smiled back at her.

Ready? Ready. For something truly sensational.

Sophie gave the gentlest nudge to one of the stacks on the balcony wall in front of her.

Some of the first students to appear, already stooping to inspect the leaflets outside their halls, cried out in surprise as still more pages cascaded down through the wide open space. And a shrill male voice far below echoed up louder than any of the others, piercing Sophie as if through her heart:

'Stop! Stay right there!'

LOCKDOWN

Sophie checked her urge to run. Then she remembered: the key!

She could not afford to be caught with that key in her pocket. If it was traced back to the studio, all the White Rose's equipment would be found, and any number of other people could be implicated. But what could she do about that now?

'Don't move! You're under arrest!'

The rasping voice was closer. Its owner had to be climbing the stairs. Maybe that gave Sophie just enough of a window to dash into the female restroom behind her? Spinning away from a puzzled-looking Hans she did just that, tossed the key down a toilet – and was back beside him, suitcase in hand, when the shouting man heaved his short overweight frame up the last few stairs.

And in that moment Sophie had a second sickening memory flash: of Hans absently slipping Christel's draft leaflet into his pocket after breakfast. She prayed to God he had ditched it since.

'You!' The unshaven man jabbed his finger at them while fighting for breath. 'You're up to no good! I saw you push the papers! I'm taking you straight to the boss. Come! *Come!*'

It was Schmid, the building's oily janitor, who saw himself as a kind of guard dog. Sophie had never heard anyone with a good word for him. The rank stench of his sweat hit her from fifteen paces.

He catapulted himself forward, seized them both by the arm and – loyal Nazi Party member that he was – began to hustle them back down the first flight of stairs.

Hans made an attempt to shrug him off, laughing and saying he had the wrong people, but when Schmid seized him with more force, he shrugged and went along with it. Sophie too let herself be led.

'Lock the doors!' Schmid yapped as other staff members ran into view. 'Lock all exits! There may be more. Let no one escape!'

At the lower levels he had to use Hans and Sophie like battering rams to barge a way through crowds of stunned-looking students, many of them quickly dropping the leaflets they'd picked up. One of those looking on in amazement and alarm from a lecture-hall doorway was Kurt Huber, the man who had written them.

When Schmid bundled them as far as the building superintendent's office, his boss was already outside, casting his eyes over the Prof's blistering words.

'I caught them!' Schmid crowed in triumph. 'They're up to no good. I saw them! Me!' His grip on Sophie's upper arm tightened in his excitement. Shouts rang out as doors were slammed and bolted.

'Make sure every last one of these is picked up,' said the livid superintendent, handing the leaflet to a secretary and ignoring Schmid except to say, 'Get them to the rector.'

Hans dug in his heels as they set off again. 'This is absurd!' he protested, still smiling. 'You have no right to arrest us.'

Sophie took courage from how relaxed Hans now seemed. Then she felt a fierce jolt as Schmid propelled them on down the corridor, past further lines of stupefied students and lecturers, to bring them before the SS officer who held total power in the university.

Rector Wüst's large office seemed full of air and light. The uniformed man himself was at his desk, a leaflet in one hand, a telephone pressed to his ear with the other. Despite his own high Nazi ranking, he'd decided at once that Gestapo HQ should be called. Sophie gathered this from his conversation while she and Hans were relieved of their bags and made to sit next to each other.

On top of the desk were two piles of already-retrieved leaflets. Some of the men moving about the office threw confused glances from the papers to the siblings then back again. In a corner, Schmid repeated how fearlessly he had 'captured the smear campaigners', wondering out loud how soon he could claim his reward.

When Wüst at last looked their way, the pupils of his eyes were like razors. But all he did was shake his head, and at that point three new men arrived.

From where she sat, Sophie had the better view of the Gestapo trio sweeping into the room with a flurry of 'Heil Hitler's. In the lead was someone she thought looked familiar. A thick-set middle-aged investigator with a hat worn low over his eyes and a red bow tie under his sombre-coloured overcoat.

'Robert Mohr,' he announced to Wüst, waving his ID. Sophie hadn't been wrong: she'd seen him sniffing around the bookshop.

For a short while, with his back to the siblings, he conversed with Schmid too softly for her to be able to hear much of what he said. But she heard Schmid yap 'reward' three times, and even from behind she could see how impatient that made the Gestapo man.

Then Mohr turned, approached them, and quite politely asked to see their identification papers. On finding them in order and handing them back, he looked closely at Hans. For a moment the older man's expression seemed to soften, and Sophie thought there wasn't a total absence of kindness in his eyes.

'You study here?' Mohr asked her brother.

'Yes, sir. Medicine. When I am not away at the Front.'

'You have served the Fatherland?'

'I have, sir, as medical back-up. In France and in the East.'

Mohr turned to cast a long, disparaging look at Schmid, who had doubtless never seen action anywhere. Plainly Mohr knew this janitor's type – one that could seldom be trusted – and lounging so casually on his seat, hand in pocket, Hans looked a picture of innocence. But Sophie still had concerns about what might be in that pocket, and when Mohr looked his way again, he too frowned.

With his gimlet eye he had spotted two small torn corners of paper flutter down behind Hans's chair.

'What are you shredding there?' Mohr demanded, pointing, and without waiting for an answer one of his men shot forward to wrestle Hans's fist out of his pocket.

He prised it apart to find what was screwed up inside. To Sophie's horror it was Christel's draft for leaflet seven, still partly intact, plus many torn fragments.

She closed her eyes. How could Hans possibly account for this?

'It's written by hand,' said the officer, passing it to Mohr, who smoothed it out then looked at Hans for an explanation.

Hans gave a sigh, appearing no less casual or confident. 'Oh, that?' he said. 'Well, we got knocked all over the place when we were being led here. I felt someone push something into my pocket.' He nodded meaningfully up at Schmid. 'Planted it, maybe? I don't even know what it is. I just guessed it might make me look guilty if I didn't get rid of it now.'

Mohr folded the paper and slipped it into his coat pocket. 'Take them into protective custody,' he ordered.

Hans and Sophie were made to stand and put their arms behind them, then handcuffed, before they were muscled out into the corridor and marched towards the exit.

With the building still in lockdown, multitudes of students and staff stood close to the walls and watched, wide-eyed. Briefly the sunlight outside dazzled Sophie before she and Hans were pushed into the back of a windowless grey van and driven away.

The journey to Gestapo HQ was short. After being booked in at the desk and handing over their personal belongings, they were led off separately to be finger-printed and photographed for the records.

In each room Sophie was taken to, and along each corridor, she noticed everyone seemed to have at least half an ear on the voice that came snarling from the radio – that of the Nazis' most venomous speechmaker, Joseph Goebbels. After the catastrophe at Stalingrad, this was the day earmarked for him to rouse the German people to even greater sacrifices. From the Sports Palace in Berlin, his message now rang out around the nation:

'I ask you,' he roared. 'Will you follow our *Führer* through thick and thin in the struggle to win this war?'

'*Ja!*' boomed his live audience, and all of Sophie's captors nodded in eager agreement. Then one of them, a uniformed officer holding a box camera, ordered her to look straight into the lens.

'Do you want a war more total than anything we can even imagine today?' demanded Goebbels.

'*Ja! Ja!...*'

'Straight into the lens!' Sophie was ordered again. And with the camera flash disguising any faint movement of her lips, Sophie murmured her own determined reply to Goebbels, to Hitler, and to every other Nazi the length and breadth of Germany:

'*Nein.*' No.

Then she was frogmarched to her cell.

DEATH CANDIDATE

When the suspect named Sophie Scholl was led into his interrogation office, Robert Mohr gave her a long hard look from his desk before dismissing the guard and inviting her to sit.

In the university rector's office he'd been shocked to find a girl there, and sitting so eerily composed as well; so shocked, in fact, that he'd insisted on interviewing her alone, with just a female stenographer taking shorthand notes at the back of the room. Meanwhile her brother would be dealt with next door – that impressive young soldier who, despite the business with the shredded sheet, had so reminded Mohr of his own uniformed son.

He took a cigarette from his silver case and lit it. Once the suspect took her seat in front of him, a great stillness descended on the simply-furnished room. But beyond it the enquiries of Mohr's special task force had gone into overdrive – so already he had a full working picture of the Scholls' friendship network in Munich, and interviews were being conducted throughout the neighbourhood.

'You were carrying a suitcase at the university?' he began.

'Yes, sir.'

'An empty suitcase?'

'It was empty because I was going home to Ulm and I planned to bring clean laundry back in it.'

'Why go in the middle of the week, when you have lectures?'

'I just heard my mother is ill, sir. I was going at short notice.'

'Then why were you at the university?'

'Because previously I'd made an arrangement to have lunch with a friend. I wanted to let her know I wouldn't be able to make it.'

Mohr picked up a pen. 'Give me the name of this friend.'

'Gisela. Gisela Schertling.'

That name was included on the list in front of him.

'And why were you accompanied by your brother?'

'I had no money, sir, for the train fare, so he was going to get me some cash at the bank. He was on his way to a lecture.'

She could not have looked more unflustered. If anything, she seemed slightly amused by it all. But she wasn't ill-mannered, nor was her brother. They had been well brought up, even if the archive showed her father hadn't always been the most loyal of citizens. It still seemed frankly incredible to Mohr that after so many months he was now at last looking into the face of the enemy he'd been searching for.

'The janitor saw you distributing leaflets,' he went on.

'No, sir. He said he saw us push them from the balcony.'

'And you did this?'

She shook her head. 'We had nothing at all to do with any leaflets. The man made a mistake. He was looking up, and sunlight was pouring in through the glass roof. He didn't know who he saw.'

Again Mohr looked at her long and hard. She met his gaze without batting an eyelid.

'You had nothing at all to do with the leaflets?'

She shrugged. 'I don't even know what they're about.'

Mohr signalled to the stenographer to bring one across. He watched the student's fresh, unemotional face as in no particular hurry she began to read it through.

He didn't need reminding that the janitor's account could not be relied on. For a reward or a promotion, such a man might say anything. But whereas the university rector had immediately swallowed his story – which was partly why this girl had been placed in a shared 'death candidate' cell where the lights would burn all night to add to her problems – Mohr was paid not to jump to conclusions.

Still, however, he was under pressure. That much had been made clear in a recent phone call from Paul Giesler, still seething about the students' protest over his Museum speech. This case needed to be settled fast, he'd told Mohr. Whoever produced the leaflets had to be exposed and seen to suffer for it – soon.

The student finished reading and placed the leaflet on Mohr's desk. Stabbing out his cigarette, he lit a new one.

'What is your opinion of this leaflet?' he asked.

'It's very well written.'

Mohr raised an eyebrow. 'You sympathize?'

'No. Just its language – it flows well.'

This girl was such a child. She imagined he had asked her for a comment on its literary quality, as one of her teachers might.

'These are not your views?'

'No.'

'You neither wrote nor distributed this leaflet, nor any others like it?'

'No.'

Mohr took a breath and consulted his pocket watch. These were surely not the perpetrators. He had felt this way since first setting eyes on them. The girl had no criminal record whatever, and no new evidence against either of them had been phoned through from the external interviews. The National Socialist state actually needed smart youngsters of their sort. As the *Führer* himself had phrased it: *Whoever has the youth has the future*.

But these things had to be done by the book.

Mohr reached for the file on her family, opened it and prepared to grill her on every last aspect of her life until he was satisfied she could be released.

The questioning lasted five hours.

Intermittently Mohr would leave to check on his colleague's progress next door with Hans Scholl. Nothing he learned caused him to revise his original hunch. The two siblings' stories about their activities that day tallied. Further back, Mohr uncovered no suggestion of treason in thought or deed. To cap it all, throughout his careful probing – occasionally raising his voice in apparent fury just as a tactic to unsettle her – the young woman maintained her cool, calm, assured manner.

Only once, when Mohr came back from comparing notes with her brother's interrogator, did she falter slightly. Mohr saw her glance wanly at the door connecting the rooms. It took him a while to get her to admit that she was concerned about her brother. Not about herself, but him. This was because, she said, she'd heard that some Gestapo officers used torture.

Mohr went back to the door and clasped the handle.

'You fear that your brother is being ill-treated?' he asked. '"Enhanced interrogation techniques" – yes?'

Before she could reply, he quickly opened and closed the door, allowing her to glimpse the other suspect sitting in a chair similar to her own, quite unmarked and in full conversational flow.

'You don't want to believe everything you hear,' Mohr told her, resuming his seat.

'No, sir,' she replied with a shy smile. 'None of us should.'

Mohr sat back, reached for his cigarette case, looked across at the suspect, then offered it first to her.

She thanked him but shook her head.

'You will return to your cell for something to eat,' Mohr said. 'A report of our conversation will be typed up for you to sign.' He paused to light his cigarette. 'Maybe you will still then have time to catch an evening train to Ulm.'

Again she thanked him, and was led away.

Mohr sat and smoked his cigarette thoughtfully before crossing to the windows and closing the blinds. Then he took off his jacket, draped it over a chair, and was washing his face and hands at the sink in the corner of the room when his external telephone rang.

'GIVE ME THE TRUTH!'

Sophie was not long in her cell before she was recalled. That didn't bother her much, since at least she'd had time to eat.

She was sharing the cell with a fellow-prisoner called Else, who was made to do odd jobs around the building by day and then locked up at night. Else liked to talk, and Sophie felt sure anything she herself said would soon find its way back to Mohr. It was actually quite a relief to get away from her.

But as soon as she re-entered Mohr's office – lit now just by the lamps on his desk and that of the stenographer – she noticed a change in the atmosphere. Jaw clenched, she resumed her seat.

All Mohr's attention was on a sheet of paper that looked a bit like a jigsaw. Sophie realized it was

Christel's handwritten draft for leaflet seven, clumsily glued together, but not clumsily enough to stop Mohr from reading it aloud now for her to listen to.

He began in a low growl which gathered in strength until on reaching the final paragraph, his shouted words ricocheted in outrage around the darkened room:

'*Today, Germany is completely encircled just as Stalingrad was. Will all Germans be sacrificed to the forces of hatred and destruction? Sacrificed to the man who persecuted the Jews, who eradicated half the Poles, and who wanted to annihilate Russia?*'

With one finger Mohr loosened the collar beneath his bow tie. 'You have heard all that before?' he asked.

'No.'

'This was to be the next resistance leaflet?'

'I don't know.'

'But you do know the person who wrote it?'

Sophie frowned. 'How could I?'

Mohr's eyes narrowed at her through the coils of his cigarette smoke. 'Because in searching your apartment, personal letters to your brother, written by this same person, have been found.'

Sophie felt her colour rise. Glaring at her, Mohr reached into a drawer, his swastika lapel badge flashing in the desk lamp's light. He held up one of Christel's chatty letters to Hans.

'The name of this person is Christoph Probst. He signs himself Christel. You know him?'

Sophie cleared her throat. 'Yes. But—'

'We also found in your brother's room a typewriter, of exactly the sort on which the previous leaflets were produced.' He reached again into the drawer. 'Then there were these.' He laid a sheaf of red postage stamps on the desk between them, and set alongside it two opened envelopes from the White Rose's mailouts that had been handed in to the Gestapo. The stamps on them matched those in the sheaf.

'This is just a coincidence,' said Sophie flatly. 'We need those stamps to write letters to all our friends and family.'

Shaking his head, Mohr put a finger to his lips. He balanced his cigarette on the ashtray's rim, then put both elbows on the desk and clasped his hands.

'Thanks to our enquiries, we now know a great deal more about you, your brother and your circle. We know, for example, that you go in and out of a certain studio—'

'Yes, because a painter we know is working there. We go to look at his pictures, and to show them to our friends.'

'Remain silent until asked to speak!'

Mohr's cheeks shook as he shouted, and Sophie saw that whereas before he may just have been pretending to be angry, he really was on a short fuse now. Probably he felt she'd made him look foolish by almost getting him to release her. But soon he recomposed himself.

'You have been lying,' he went on. 'You and whoever else is involved are enemies of Germany and its people. I need the truth. This interview will continue until I get it.'

Sophie knew what she had to do.

Hans would be doing the same thing next door. If Willi, Schurik, Christel or even the Prof had already fallen into the net, then so too would they: first deny everything, then take all the blame. Sometimes in the last few months she'd idly wondered how she might perform at such a moment. Although she had always imagined it *as* just a moment.

But this went on for hour, after hour, after hour.

Mohr kept leaving the room to consult with colleagues. Now and then he'd return with fresh pieces of evidence: a new informer had said Sophie never gave the 'Heil Hitler' salute; a duplicating machine, covered in fingerprints, had been discovered in the studio cellar...

Yet Sophie batted back whatever Mohr threw at her. She surprised even herself by her steadfastness. Calmly, convincingly, she went on claiming no knowledge of the White Rose campaign, denying that anyone she knew was involved in any way.

God perhaps had answered her prayers to grant her this strength. She felt as if four walls had risen up around her, invisible yet unbreakable, and here inside them nothing could touch her. At times between Mohr's onslaughts she even felt able to let her thoughts wander: to Ulm, her home, her parents – wondering what they might say if they knew where their daughter now sat.

But then, as if a switch had been flicked, everything changed.

'You wish to hear what your brother says now?' Mohr asked, re-taking his seat after yet another exit and waving a typed document. It was several sheets long, and as soon as Mohr read out some snatches, his words turned to a blizzard in Sophie's head.

His words, Hans's words.

Mohr was telling her that finally, in the face of unanswerable evidence, Hans had broken down and confessed. He was taking responsibility for everything: writing, printing and distributing the leaflets, even for painting the graffiti slogans. Still though, inwardly and outwardly, Sophie stayed unruffled.

'I don't believe it,' she told Mohr softly when he finished.

'Then do you believe *that*?' He slammed down the document, folded back at its last page, and stabbed his finger halfway down.

There was no doubting what Sophie saw beneath the printed words 'Read and signed by'. That was definitely Hans's signature. The ink on the page still glistened in the lamplight.

Suddenly all the air seemed to go out of the room. Again she pictured her parents back in Ulm, her father standing in the kitchen, warning her how merciless the Nazis would be.

'Give me the truth!' roared Mohr. 'He can't have done it all alone. Did you write and distribute the leaflets with your brother?'

Sophie plucked at the fabric of her skirt. The time had come to change course, yet she took her four walls with her.

'Yes I did,' she said to Mohr's face. 'And I'm proud of it!'

However long Sophie's second interrogation had lasted up to that point, it seemed to go on for twice as long afterwards.

In her heart, she'd known since stuffing her first White Rose envelope that it would end like this. To live the good life that she'd heard about in the Prof's lecture, she had come such a long way with her beloved brother. Ahead now lay the final stretch.

All of it, she insisted to Mohr, absolutely all, had been the work of just the two of them. They had written and circulated the leaflets, often by travelling to other cities to post them. They'd put up the slogans. They'd also paid for the whole White Rose operation by themselves, using her personal allowance and Hans's army pay, topped up by occasional loans. Not one other person was involved. They had not even mentioned their campaign to anyone.

Mohr's frustration mounted by the minute.

He'd prowl the floor rapping out names at Sophie – 'You must have spoken to *him*!' 'How could you not have involved *her*?' – but behind her invisible walls Sophie could not be reached.

Among many others, Mohr kept naming Schurik, Christel, Willi, Traute – but no, no, no, no, Sophie relentlessly told him. 'My brother and I are the sole culprits. There is nothing more to tell.'

At length Mohr crossed to the nearer window and wound up its blind. Grey daylight spilled in past him. So full of pent-up fury that he seemed to radiate heat, he said without turning, 'You are aware of the consequences if you insist on taking full responsibility?'

'Yes, I am.'

Mohr strode to the door, ripped it open and called the guard.

THE BLACK TRUCKS

While Sophie was losing track of the hours, Mohr had been counting off every minute. Drying his face after a shave at his office sink, he knew he would not be given much more time for cross-examination. Schäfer his chief had called him in person to make that quite clear.

In all his professional life Mohr had never known such a suspect – or to use the virtual schoolgirl's own word, 'culprit'. Seventeen hours in, he'd learned so much about her life, yet still he had so little he could use. She'd probably have been able to sit there stone-walling for weeks, months.

But though she didn't know it, Sophie did not have months or weeks left. This student plot had caused a stir at the topmost level of the party, so the cases against the accused were scheduled to be fast-tracked through a special People's Court. Arrangements had already been made for 'Blood Judge' Roland Freisler to be flown into Munich. During just the first year that he'd been serving as president of the People's Court, well over a thousand death sentences had been handed out. Now there would be more.

Mohr pulled on his shirt and peered into the mirror to knot his bow tie. The face gazing back at him looked unnerved.

Schäfer had said Giesler was clamouring for a gallows to be built on the city's central square. Then the students could be hanged by the neck in full view of everyone.

Mohr was not so sure about that. If the White Rose really had tapped into wider unrest, public executions might provoke further protest. In the aftermath of Stalingrad, these were uncertain times for the National Socialists, which was why no mercy could be shown to any who defied them.

Yet who were the White Rose's true ringleaders? Mohr refused to believe it was a girl of only twenty-one and her brother. She even still swore – laughably – that her 'Christel' had nothing to do with printing and distributing the leaflets, or with the graffiti. These three had to be a front while others pulled their strings: older men, hardened criminals, types who would think far enough ahead not to leave trails of incriminating evidence all over Munich. Youngsters like these, like his own son, had too much else on their minds.

By telephone Mohr summoned the stenographer and asked for the accused to be brought for a third, and almost certainly last, interrogation.

It was time to try breaking her in a different way.

Since the last session Sophie hadn't got much sleep. For the opening phase of Mohr's next bombardment – 'Give me names, give me names, give me names!' – she often had to blink hard to keep her eyes open.

She revived a little when the door opened and coffee was brought in for him. From its rich aroma alone, she knew it was real coffee, not the thin wartime stuff made from acorns that ordinary Germans had to make do with. She revived some more when she saw two cups with the percolator, both of which Mohr proceeded to fill.

'Go on,' he said, pushing one across to the far side of his desk. 'Drink.'

Sophie gladly obeyed. It tasted sublime. She accepted a refill too, and to her surprise Mohr gave her time to savour it in silence.

'It is well known,' he then said in a confidential way, 'that women are the weaker sex. They can be made to think, speak, and even act against their true will. Since coming to Munich, you have been a woman among men. Men with a firm idea about the world – a wrong idea, criminally wrong – and they have forced you to do their will. You simply need to say that this is so, and let us know who these men are, and things will go a lot better for you in court.'

Sophie breathed in deeply. 'No,' she said.

'"*No*"!' Mohr boomed back, rocking himself up out of his chair. He slapped the desk so hard that Sophie flinched from head to toe. '"*No*"! Is this the only word you can say? Are you not paying attention? I am giving you an opportunity to save your own neck!'

'It's not just my own neck that concerns me,' she said in a small clear voice. 'Besides, I have done nothing against my will.' She paused. 'You call my brother and me enemies of Germany and its people, but we do love this land, just not your version of it. We love the German people too, just not what you're turning them into.'

Mohr strutted to the window, shaking his head as if to get rid of a bug that had wormed its way inside. Then he swung around.

'Your idea of the world is so wrong!'

'No, sir,' Sophie answered, daring to smile. 'It's your idea that is wrong. I did what I did in the best interests of my people. I won't betray my brother and I won't betray our own, true idea.'

'Your "own true idea"! And how would you describe this idea?'

'That each of us must be free to think and act as we see fit.'

It didn't take the stenographer long to type up Sophie's confession. Before Mohr read it over and asked Sophie to sign it, he sat glowering at her from behind his desk, feeling far more exhausted and desperate than the girl before him looked.

'What did we ever do,' he asked, 'that made you hate us so?'

'"Hate" is one of your master race's words, not mine,' Sophie replied. Then she surprised him. 'But I could tell you when I began to see the darkness falling, and this was long before the war.'

'Speak,' said Mohr.

Sophie gathered herself.

'Near us in Ulm there was an institution for mentally ill children, and my mother – well, my mother heard disturbing reports of what went on there. Black trucks drawing up, taking groups of the children away, then never bringing them back.'

She fell silent. In all the hours Mohr had been with her, he'd never seen her come so close to losing her self-control.

'When more black trucks arrived, the children who were put on board asked where they were being taken. The nurses, of course, knew; these children were going to be exterminated, because your Nazis called them "useless eaters", not worth keeping alive. But to the children the nurses lied. They said, "Why, the trucks are going to carry you off to Heaven!" And so, as the vehicles drove away, the children could be heard singing with joy.'

Again she took a moment. Mohr felt driven to look away.

'Even then,' he heard Sophie conclude, 'I thought that this was becoming a country I didn't particularly want to be alive in.'

Still keeping his eyes averted, Mohr pushed across the desk the typed document along with an uncapped pen, and at the same time he picked up his phone.

'Tell the chief we're done here,' he said into the receiver.

18

FREEDOM

Sophie had spent so long facing Mohr that when she was left to stew in her cell for most of Sunday, she kept hallucinating him right in front of her. Sometimes she even recoiled from his image.

As the bright sun made its westward trek across the sky outside her high barred window, she tried to snatch a few winks of sleep. With Else regularly coming and going, that wasn't easy.

Sophie guessed her cellmate was on suicide watch – under orders to make sure Sophie didn't end her own life before the Nazi state ended it for her. Each time Else opened her mouth, Sophie suspected she'd been primed to dig more information out of her. Perhaps that wasn't always true; she did just seem to love talking, mainly – unnecessarily – about how Sophie might still be set free, and how many others inside this building were saying how courageous she was. Once, however, she passed across a scrap of news.

'They have brought in a third person from your group!' she knelt beside Sophie's bed and whispered.

Still half-asleep, Sophie only just stopped herself from incriminating anyone by blurting out a name, then she closed her eyes again. But if someone else really was now in custody, she wasn't sure who she wanted it to be. For any of the others to have to go through this would be bad; for married family men like Christel or the Prof it would be ruinous. Yet hadn't those two played too small a part to be the third suspect?

Later that Sunday, his identity was revealed.

Sophie was summoned, under the inevitable escort, to a room where a prosecutor handed her a document. Headed 'Indictment', it looked a little like a White Rose leaflet. So this was to be the full case against her. As Sophie stood glancing through it, she found it hard to take in what the seated man was saying. 'The investigation is complete,' was the gist of both the document and his words. 'You are being charged with high treason.'

There in black and white was her name on the Indictment: *Sophia Magdalena Scholl (no previous conviction)*, but what made Sophie's heart plummet was the sight of the names alongside it: Hans, which she'd expected, but also that of poor Christel.

Their threefold crime – she wasn't sure if she was reading this, hearing it, or both – was to have created an organization to carry out treason, to have assisted Germany's enemies in wartime, and to have encouraged the demoralization of Germany's armed forces.

What she definitely did hear was that their trial would take place at Munich's Palace of Justice at 10.00 a.m. the very next day. She would now be given writing materials, and she was advised to write to any loved ones immediately on returning to her cell.

To stop her hands trembling she gripped the Indictment tighter. It was, she knew, her death warrant.

Else was waiting when she got back, keen to know how it had gone. Sophie passed her the Indictment – even Else would be able to say nothing hopeful now – and went to stand beneath the window.

She imagined on this day of rest all the people strolling past outside in their Sunday best. 'Such a beautiful sunny day,' she murmured, more to God than to Else, 'and I have to go.'

Her eyes filled, the world momentarily blurred, but then she sighed and cleared her throat, bringing it all back into focus.

'Yet how many others are dying on the battle-fields?' Sophie went on, louder, wanting Else to hear this and pass it on later to whoever she reported to. 'What does my death matter, so long as what we wrote woke up thousands and stirred them to take action?'

She took a long time on her letters to her family, most of it spent thinking about them rather than writing. Back in Ulm, had news even reached them yet about her and Hans? And would they be allowed to attend the trial? All Sophie felt able to do was thank them for the love they'd always shown her, and ask their forgiveness for bringing them such pain now. But she also made it clear that faced by the Nazis, she could never have acted in any other way.

While she wrote, she had a brief visit from the counsel appointed by the court to speak in defence of the accused. Since Sophie had already admitted her guilt, he told her briskly, he could only plead that as a woman – doubtless under male influence – she might get a lighter sentence. Sophie greeted this with a dry smile.

'I am equally guilty,' she said. 'We must all be treated the same. And of course I understand there can be only one result.' She paused. 'But tell me this: as serving soldiers, do the two men not have the right to be executed by firing squad?'

Thrown into confusion by so direct a question, the counsel took off his glasses and pinched the top of his nose. 'They've been dismissed from the army,' he mumbled, unable to meet Sophie's eye.

'Then how are we all to die?' she asked, watching the blood drain out of his face. 'By hanging or beheading?'

That was too much for him. Without giving his client another look, he repacked his case and left.

Although the cell light blazed all night, after kneeling to say her prayers Sophie managed to sleep quite well, and she dreamed an unusual dream. Waiting to be taken to court next morning, she decided to share it with Else, and so too with a wider world.

'It was a sunny day,' she recounted, 'and I was carrying a child in a long white gown up a steep path to be christened. Then a crack opened up in the ground before me and I was plunged inside, but not before I had set down the child safely on the other side.'

Else searched Sophie's face for an explanation.

'The child is our idea – the White Rose's idea – and although we carriers will die, our idea will survive, and it will flourish.'

At around 9.00 a.m. two detectives from the regular police force arrived to handcuff Sophie then drive her in an unmarked car to the Palace of Justice, not far from Munich Main Station.

On the bed which she'd carefully made up, she had left her copy of the Indictment. When Else went across to look at it, she found Sophie had scrawled some private graffiti on the back.

Freiheit, it said.

Freedom.

ANOTHER KIND OF JUSTICE

They were forbidden to touch or speak, but when Sophie, Hans and Christel came together in the wood-panelled courtroom, the weary smiles they gave one another spoke volumes.

This, finally, was where their plot had led them.

Hitler and his henchmen ruled over tens of millions of Germans – plus a European empire holding hundreds of millions more – yet a few hundred words mailed out on a few thousand pieces of paper still posed a life-or-death threat to the Nazi way of life. So now, half a week after being taken into custody, three young people had to answer for it.

They were seated behind a wooden rail just around the corner from the president's bench, with armed guards posted between each of them. There was no jury, and only invited guests filled the public gallery – almost all of them in grey or brown uniforms. Any faint hope Sophie had of seeing her parents one last time evaporated.

This would not be a trial so much as a pause for breath on the way to the place of execution. The verdict was a foregone conclusion – and for the first hour and a half of the proceedings, from the moment everyone stood for the president of the court's arrival, Sophie retreated behind her own four walls.

Else had earlier tipped her off about this president, Freisler by name. He apparently had a reputation for throwing fearsome, abusive tantrums from the bench. He would tear into the accused more like a prosecutor than a judge. But just one look at him sweeping in like a pantomime Pope in his flowing red robes and matching little red hat (which on removal showed the top of his head was as bald as an egg) made Sophie want to giggle rather than tremble.

It was he who did nearly all the talking, or rather shrieking. The students' own counsel simply put on record how baffled he was that they should have done things they ought to be ashamed of.

Freisler ranted, Freisler raved. He called the three of them parasites, dogs; he leaped up and jabbed his finger at each in turn. Whenever he reached fever pitch in his ear-splitting insults, which was often, he looked as if he might pass out from sheer exertion.

Sophie sat through it all as if in a trance. It could have been a kindergarten drama performed by overgrown children. It saddened and embarrassed her that her own German language – so fine when used by writers as skilled as Heinrich Heine or Thomas Mann – could be made to sound so hideous.

In the same trance-like state she watched as the evidence against them was paraded for all to see: typewriter, duplicator, stencils and paint for the graffiti, sheets of stamps for further envelopes. Extracts from the six existing leaflets were read aloud to cries of 'Disgraceful!' from the gallery. When Christel's jigsaw draft was read out, some onlookers shook their fists at the accused.

Though each of the three was allowed to say a few words, Freisler only wanted to hear them admit they had made a terrible error. When they admitted no such thing, he kept interrupting so ferociously that nobody could hear them anyway. Yet Sophie did squeeze in one remark that brought gasps from every corner.

'Many people think like us,' she boldly told the president. 'They just don't dare to speak. Now someone has made a start.'

Several times she caught Mohr watching her closely from his seat. In a way Sophie pitied him, just as she pitied all those like him: without the freedom to think or act for themselves they were hardly human, just parts of a machine, able only to obey orders.

Mohr was not asked to address the court. A short summary of the results of the Gestapo investigation was read out instead by his chief inspector. And when the time came for 'last words' from the accused, Christel alone thought it worth trying to speak. Soon enough, however, he was again shouted down.

These were not ears the White Rose could ever have reached, nor hearts they could ever unlock. Sophie understood that this trial simply had to be endured, but when news of it spread, then the White Rose idea would be communicated to countless others.

The prosecutor, of course, called for the death penalty, and after ninety minutes of the charade, the president of the court and his colleagues withdrew to consider their verdict over lunch.

Sophie, Hans and Christel were not scheduled to eat. Made to stay in their seats, they were watched with venom by those in the gallery. Meanwhile janitor Schmid, buttoned up in a Sunday suit for his non-speaking role as star witness, basked in glory as the uniformed men reached over to shake his hand and slap their 'national comrade' on the back.

At one point Sophie dared to crane her neck around the policeman beside her and she caught

Hans's eye. Wryly she raised an eyebrow. In reply Hans pulled up his grubby shirt to his nose and pretended to find the smell bad, reminding her they'd been wearing the same clothes since Thursday. Sophie swallowed a smile.

The president at last returned and prepared to pronounce his verdict, a party piece he clearly relished. When he stood and replaced his absurd hat, everyone else had to rise too. But he'd only just begun to speak when a scuffle in the doorway silenced him.

There were comments from the gallery, then some shouting. Two civilians were forcing their way in past the guards.

Sophie snapped out of her trance. The two people were her parents.

Somehow amid all the confusion her father succeeded in battling his way through to the courtroom floor. She tried to go out to him but was roughly pushed back by the police officer.

'I am here to defend my children!' she heard her father cry to their counsel. 'Go ask the president of the court if I may speak.'

To her astonishment the counsel went up to the bench, and for several seconds he and the scowling Freisler were locked in hushed conversation. Urgently Sophie tried to meet her father's eye, to show him how calm and resolved she was, but the dear man was really too frantic to be able to see anyone.

Then Freisler shot out a red-robed arm as if aiming a punch at the counsel. 'Get them out of my court!' he screamed at the guards, who raced at once up to Father Scholl, seized him and began to hustle him away. Sophie's mother was already out of sight.

'One day there will be another kind of justice!' the large old man bellowed at the president, pointing his finger heavenwards. And before he was bundled out and the door shut on him, he declared to everybody present, 'My children shall go down in history!'

It was hard to imagine Freisler looking any madder than he had all morning, but now his anger went off the scale. After spitting out the names of Sophie, Hans and Christel, he screeched the only words with which this farce could be allowed to end:

'For committing acts of high treason, and for attempting to destroy the German people's National Socialist way of life, you are sentenced to death!'

Aware most eyes were on her, Sophie kept a neutral expression. Death: just for saying she believed in something different. She was glad that at least her parents hadn't had to hear that. And yet despite their public show of support, she did wonder how they really felt, deep down, about the way she and Hans had behaved.

Freisler turned to the police. 'Away with them to Stadelheim Prison!' And as the three were being manacled before their transfer to Munich's southern suburbs, Hans nodded up at the departing Blood Judge.

'Today it's us,' he called out, loudly enough for Freisler to glance back, startled, over his shoulder. 'Tomorrow it will be you.'

A DOORWAY TO ETERNITY

Sophie's cell on Death Row at Stadelheim was bleaker than the one back at Gestapo HQ. But at least as prisoner #526 she didn't have to share it with anyone else.

She'd not yet been told how long she would have to wait before her sentence was carried out. The fact that she was still in her own clothes, not the striped uniform of the convict, suggested it wouldn't be any time soon. From Else she'd learned that most prisoners could expect to spend at least three months here. Even so, when she heard the turning of keys to open her cell door, she got to her feet and braced herself.

'You have visitors,' said the female warder without looking at her. 'Come.'

Puzzled, since she'd been told no visits would be allowed, Sophie followed her along the dimly-lit corridor.

In a small featureless room she found both her parents standing on the far side of a wooden barrier. Sophie stiffened. Face to face like this, they'd surely let rip at her for ruining not just her own life but theirs as well. Any parent would.

At first all they could do was stare at one another in different kinds of disbelief. Her mother had plainly been crying but was holding it together now, and Sophie longed for that to continue.

'They had the humanity to let us in,' said her father at last, hardly able to open his mouth for emotion. 'We've seen Hans. I told him how proud we are of you both. You did the right thing.'

Sophie blinked with relief.

'Hans didn't want any of these,' her mother added, holding a small paper bag above the barrier. 'Would you like them, Sophie?'

A guard stepped forward to inspect the contents, then passed it back to Sophie.

'Sweets!' she said, starting to grin. 'I didn't get any lunch, so thank you!'

Her mother spoke again, so softly that it was more like thinking out loud. 'Sophie, Sophie, to think you'll never be coming through the door again!'

Sophie clutched the sweet bag hard. Her smile did

not waver. 'Ah,' she said, 'but what are a few more little years here anyway?'

Her deeply religious mother nodded. She knew all about life being nothing more than a doorway to eternity. 'Sophie...' she still murmured, her voice beginning to break. 'You will remember Jesus?'

'Yes,' Sophie assured her. 'Yes I will. And so must you!'

Someone behind Sophie announced the interview was over.

She reached up and managed to grasp the hands of both her parents before she was led back out into the corridor's shadows.

Her smile remained fixed until she had to wait for her cell door to be unlocked. Only then did the pain she'd seen in her parents' expressions become too great for her to bear.

Her shoulders sagged, her eyes stung, and for the first time since her ordeal began, the private walls all around her seemed in danger of tumbling down.

At precisely that moment, Robert Mohr – in Stadelheim on other business – walked into view. Never having seen Sophie moved to tears by either sorrow or fear, he checked his step – and that was all Sophie needed to shore herself up again.

'I've just said goodbye to my parents,' she explained, drying her eyes with the back of one hand. 'You understand?'

Some of the colour left Mohr's face as he watched her being re-admitted to her cell.

'Yes,' he said before she was locked back inside. 'Yes, I do.'

Little more than an hour later, at 4.00 p.m. Sophie was led from her cell a second time. This interview was even briefer. On her return, Sophie wondered if she'd been hallucinating again.

In a room filled with witnesses she'd been informed that there was to be no pardon for her, therefore 'justice would take its course' at 5.00 p.m. that same day.

It was no mere figment of her imagination, though – as Sophie had to accept when the final knock came at the door. While she was being conducted from the cell she made herself think only of the fortifying verses at the opening of the 90th Psalm:

Lord, thou hast been our dwelling place in all generations.

Before the mountains were brought forth, or ever thou hadst formed the earth and the world, even from everlasting to everlasting, thou art God.

On account of some words written on paper, Sophie Scholl was condemned to die decades before her time. But God's words were inscribed on her heart, and now – regretting nothing, hoping only that the White Rose's torch would start to banish the Nazi night – they helped her face without fear her journey towards eternity.

Less than a minute passed between Sophie leaving her cell at five o'clock that afternoon and the moment her life ended.

Fifty steps from the main cell block stood a much smaller, single-storey building. Straight-backed, without hesitation, Sophie walked under escort across the courtyard and into it.

She was awaited by several servants of the Nazi state. Asked to identify herself, she did so in a firm voice. As her sentence was read out again, she saw awaiting her in the next whitewashed room a man of middling height in a long black coat, white gloves, white shirt, a black bow tie and a tall black top hat.

When Sophie was brought forward, this man – who was her executioner, and would soon be Hans's and Christel's – pulled aside a black curtain to reveal an upright wooden frame inside which was suspended a razor-sharp blade. Two assistants led Sophie, a perfectly healthy young woman not yet twenty-two years of age, to the guillotine and held her in place.

In the unforgiving words of the report written by the prosecutor – one of a handful of official witnesses – the executioner *then released the blade, which immediately severed the head of the condemned from her trunk. The prison doctor confirmed that death had occurred. The condemned was calm and collected.*

* * *

Moments earlier, out on a nearby Munich street that he still had the freedom to walk, Robert Mohr came to a halt when he heard a bell toll five o'clock. As if in response to an order, he removed his hat and bowed his head.

There, at the going down of the sun on 22nd February 1943, with pedestrians swarming all around him on the pavement, Mohr stood for a full minute as a voice went on sounding in his head: the voice of a girl saying no with all her heart. 'Now someone has made a start,' Sophie Scholl had told the court – and neither Robert Mohr nor anyone else could tell where this might end.

He then resumed his journey back to Gestapo HQ, but some of the life had gone out of him too.

NOT FORGOTTEN

WHAT HAPPENED NEXT …

LIKE A SECRET LIGHT

Good, splendid young people! You shall not have died in vain; you shall not be forgotten.

So said one of Germany's greatest writers, Thomas Mann, about Sophie, Hans and Christel. He was speaking in a radio broadcast for German listeners, which he made from abroad in June 1943 after hearing news of the first three White Rose executions.

The war, however, went on. By the time the Nazis were at last overthrown and peace was restored to Europe, in May 1945, Sophie would have been celebrating her twenty-fourth birthday. By then, the six core members of the White Rose group – Sophie, Hans, Christel, Alexander 'Schurik' Schmorell, Willi Graf and Professor Kurt Huber – had all long since been tracked down and executed. No one can say for sure how many others died in the global struggle we now call World War Two, but estimates begin at well over 50 million people.

After crushing the White Rose group, the Nazi state did everything it could to stop news of their plot from spreading, for fear that many other Germans might welcome their demands for peace and freedom. Yet those demands still got through. Once leaflet six had been smuggled out of Germany, it was reprinted by the ten thousand and dropped into German cities by Allied bomber planes.

The members of the White Rose group were not the only Germans who dared to say *no* to the Nazis. There are rousing stories of other individuals and groups who spoke out for what they believed in, then usually lost their lives. But the almost incredibly brave example set by the White Rose plotters captured in a special way the imaginations of those who had to live under Nazi rule – people like the poet Ilse Aichinger, who was the same age as Sophie in 1943.

An inexpressible hope leaped up in me... Ilse wrote about the time during the war when she heard of the White Rose, *and I was not the only one who felt this way... This hope – which made it possible for us to go on living – was not just the hope for our survival... It helped so many that still had to die: even they could die with hope... It was like a secret light that expanded over the land: it was joy.*

* * *

Today the White Rose's campaign is remembered in Germany with pride and gratitude. In a major German TV series of 2003, Sophie and Hans Scholl were voted fourth equal by the public in a list of the greatest Germans of all time. Elsewhere in the world, the example set by White Rose members is an inspiration to anyone who believes all people should be free to think and act as they see fit. The name of Sophie Scholl in particular – the group's only female core member in a wartime world run very much by men – still rings out. *He who does not act does not exist*, wrote the philosopher Gottfried Leibniz – and although Sophie cruelly lost her life when she was so young, she exists in our minds for ever through acting as she did.

TIMELINE

1933 Nazi Party led by Adolf Hitler comes to power. Soon no other parties are permitted. Gestapo is formed to eliminate opposition, while Nazis set out to bring all German people in other European countries under their rule

1938 On *Kristallnacht* ('Crystal Night' or the Night of Broken Glass) Nazis organize destruction of 7,500 Jewish shops in Germany and burning of 400 synagogues. Such actions anticipate the Holocaust, the Nazi slaughter of 6 million Jews in German-occupied Europe

1939 World War Two begins with Nazi Germany invading Poland

1940 Nazi Germany occupy Denmark, Norway, Holland, Belgium and France

1941 Nazi German invasion of Russia begins in June. In December, war is declared on the United States of America

1942 Sophie Scholl arrives in Munich to study at University

1943 Nazi German armies surrender at Stalingrad, Russia. Nazis now in retreat

1944 Hitler survives assassination plot organized by German military leaders

1945 Russian troops enter Nazi Germany in January. By early May Germany surrenders unconditionally to Allies, with Hitler taking his own life in late April. 'Victory in Europe Day' is celebrated every year afterwards on 8 May – just one day before Sophie Scholl's date of birth on 9 May.

HISTORICAL CONTEXTS

Allied forces: Troops of countries opposing Nazi Germany and its partners (Italy and Japan) in World War Two. At first, the Allies were France, Poland, Britain and the countries of the British Empire, such as India. Soon they were joined by countries of the British Commonwealth like Canada and Australia. The state known in 1939 as the Soviet Union, of which Russia was the main part, initially entered into a partnership with Nazi Germany but in June 1941 the Nazis invaded the Soviet Union, which then joined the Allies. Later still, the Allies were joined by other countries like The Netherlands, Belgium, Greece and Yugoslavia. The United States assisted the Allies from 1939 and officially joined them after the Japanese attack on Pearl Harbor, the US naval base, in December 1941.

Balalaika: A guitar-like instrument with a triangular body popular in Russia.

Beresina: A river of strategic importance in Russia where fighting took place as the Soviet forces drove the Nazis westwards. It was also the site of a famous battle in 1813, often remembered as an invasion which turned into a disaster, when the Russians drove Napoleon's French army out of Russia.

Duplicating machine: A machine the size of a large typewriter which printed copies of the White Rose leaflets.

Führer: The German word for 'Leader', used by Hitler from 1921 to describe himself as leader of the Nazi party and later used by many to refer to Hitler's leadership of the German people.

Gestapo: The Nazi secret police, used for security purposes throughout German-occupied territory. The word is an abbreviation of the German words for Secret State Police.

Heil Hitler salute: The famous stiff-armed salute made with the right hand, used as a greeting in Nazi Germany. 'Heil Hitler' means 'Hail (or give praise) to Hitler'. Often people said 'Heil Hitler' while they made the salute.

Iron Cross: One of the highest honours awarded by the Nazis for outstanding military endeavours. It was a medal in the shape of a black cross, with a swastika at its centre, on a ribbon of red and black.

National Socialist Party (Nazis): The political party led by Hitler which came to power in Germany in 1933. 'Nazi' was how English-speakers abbreviated its full title, 'National Socialist German Worker's Party'.

Russian Front (Eastern Front): The 'Eastern Front' in World War Two refers to the parts of Eastern Europe and Russia where the forces of Nazi Germany clashed with the Allies, mainly the forces of the Soviet Union. The most intense fighting was in Russia itself – which is why Germans referred to it as 'the Russian Front'.

Spitzel: Police informers, including young people, who were encouraged or forced by the Nazis to report anti-Nazi behaviour.

Stadelheim Prison: The main prison in Munich, one of the largest prisons in Germany. Hitler himself had been imprisoned there in 1922 for assaulting a political rival.

Stalingrad, Battle of: One of the most important battles in World War Two, fought for over five months between late August 1942 and early February 1943, in which the Soviet Russians eventually defeated the Nazis. In terms of troop numbers it was the largest battle in the war – and in fact the largest battle in the history of warfare. It represented a great turning point, since after this battle the Nazis were in long-term retreat.

Stormtroopers: Members of a long-standing semi-military wing of the Nazi political party – called 'brownshirts' because of their uniform, and widely feared.

Swastika: A geometrical figure that became associated with the Nazis, who made it their badge and put it on their flags and armbands. They took it from ancient eastern cultures, where it had been used as a symbol of good luck. 'Swastika' comes from the Sanskrit (ancient Indian) word meaning 'to promote well-being'.

Yellow star: The notorious badge which the Nazis forced Jewish people to wear to identify themselves during the war – a Star of David (made of two intersecting triangles) coloured yellow and often bearing the word 'Jude' (Jew) in the middle.

INCREDIBLE PEOPLE DOING INCREDIBLE THINGS

The most thrilling stories in history